Launch Pad: The Countdown to Writing Your Book

Emma Dhesi

Grace Sammon

Launch Pad: The Countdown to Writing Your Book

Copyright © 2023 by Emma Dhesi and Grace Sammon

All rights reserved.

Published by Red Penguin Books

Bellerose Village, New York

Library of Congress Control Number:

ISBN

Print 978-1-63777-370-3

Digital 978-1-63777-369-7

The views and opinions expressed are those of the individual authors and do not necessarily reflect the views and opinions of the book sponsors.

Contents

Foreword
by Amy Ferris

Words.

They can lift you, inspire you, move you, rattle you.

They can shape you, mold you, flatten you, devastate you.

They can cut you deep.

They can rip you to shreds.

They can make you brave.

They can fill you with courage.

They can haunt you forever.

They can hold you up or hold you back.

They can stop you dead in your tracks, or make you jump for joy.

They can let you go, or let you in.

They can relieve you, encourage you, enlighten you, enliven you.

They can be engraved or tattooed; promised or broken.

They can fill you with hope, with worry, with sorrow, with grace.

They can make you taller, and stronger and kinder and more generous.

They can melt your heart. Change your heart. Break your heart. Mend your heart.

They can anger you. Enrage you. Send chills up your spine.

They can fill you to the brim with goodness.

They can carry you, calm you, caress you and challenge you.

They can make you feel like a million bucks, or be offered up as two cents.

They are spoken, written, whispered, signed, danced to, silenced, shouted, screamed. They are shared, spilled, scattered, sung, performed.

They form sentences and paragraphs; poems and sonnets.

They are plagiarized, minimized, maximized, hyphenated, and sized to your favorite font. They are on cards and mugs ... and yes, a picture can be worth a thousand of them.

They can wish you well or wish you gone.

They can fill a thousand pages or a post-it.

They can move the universe.

They can shake your soul.

They can change your mind.

They can make you weep.

They can make you proud.

They can be bold and audacious; cruel and nasty, and yes, they can put the fear of God in you.

They can sting you, or heal you.

They can whip you into shape or soothe your weary tired soul.

They can be forgiven but not forgotten.

They can be recited, memorized, remembered, recalled.

They can be tucked away for years and suddenly a memory.

They can make you cower or crawl; stand tall or stand up.

They can change you forever.

They can make you feel like you swallowed the sun.

They can save your life.

Amy Ferris is an **author, editor, screenwriter, and playwright**. She has contributed to numerous magazines and literary anthologies, and her memoir Marrying George Clooney: Confessions From a Midlife Crisis was adapted into an off-Broadway play in 2012.

She is best found on FB: https://www.facebook.com/amy.ferris

Introduction

When Grace Sammon approached me about pulling together an anthology for novelists, particularly first-time novelists, I jumped at the opportunity because 'first-timers' are exactly who I have made it my mission to help launch.

It's no secret that writing your first novel is a tricky business. It's like a 1,000-piece jigsaw puzzle that takes time and effort to put together. You can start with the corners and the outer edges but, when it comes to the inner puzzle pieces, that's when things get difficult. Even for more developed authors, it's the fine-tuning and skill development that brings quality to our craft.

Grace and I wanted to offer all authors the written equivalent of the picture on the front of the jigsaw puzzle box with Launch Pad: The Countdown To Writing Your Book.

The aim of this book is to give you a structured approach to your writing. We have ordered the book so you can go through it chapter by chapter, adding to your plot, your characters, your scenes and complete skill set, so that by the end of the book, you have a concrete and clearly defined writing process, as well as the helpful countdown lists.

We start by looking at research and outlining, then take you through scene structure and how to add suspense to your scenes. In Chapter 5, we help you "world build" (and that's not just for sci-fi or historical novels!).

The Top Ten Countdown at the end of each chapter is to ensure you have the practical steps needed to implement what you learnt in each chapter. For, as you know, it's one thing to read the theory of something, it's another to put it into practice. We want you to cement your new knowledge and up-level your skill set.

In pulling this anthology together, I sought the people I knew were best placed to talk about each subject. For example, Samantha Skal specialises in how to write suspense that works across all genres. Stacy Juba is a seasoned editor who, as a published author herself, knows exactly what you need to make your novel engaging and forward moving. Janyre Tromp has had years of experience working for and with agents, and is best placed to give you the steps you need to get your novel publisher-ready.

As each of the chapters dropped into my inbox, clear themes emerged. The first was the importance of understanding your genre. I know that, as a new writer, this won't be top of your mind in the beginning, but if you study and get to know the genre in which you're writing early on, you'll put yourself in pole position to write a compelling and unputdownable novel.

Genre, as you will discover, is important because readers have expectations from the books they read. That can be as simple as a romance novel having a happily ever after, a thriller having at least one twist at the end, or a fantasy novel using magical elements. And, of course, each genre has its own tropes and expectations which you need to include if you're going to write a book people want to read.

The second theme that emerged was that your novel needs to have a very clear and logical cause-and-effect trajectory. Nowhere is this more clearly identified than in Joe Bunting's chapter on scene structure.

You'll also see this in Carol Van Den Hende's chapter on point of view and Heather Davis' chapter on show and tell.

What each of these chapters shows is that logic must prevail. There needs to be a reason why your character does what they do and says what they say.

When your reader understands these things, then they can relate to and empathise with your character (even if that character is unlikeable).

The third theme that emerged from the craft chapters is that, once you have a clear cause-and-effect trajectory for your storyline, you then put it on the page.

In your head, you know exactly what happens and probably can see the facial expressions of your characters, but your reader cannot. Unless you tell your reader what the character is thinking or feeling and how they are physically moving within a scene, you will leave them floundering.

At every stage of the writing process, you must put your character's world on the page. You'll see this reflected in Kat Caldwell's chapter on character development, Heather Davis' chapter on show and tell, as well as my chapter about working with a book coach (whose job it is to make sure you put it on the page!).

A quick note on style: As Janyre Tromp mentions in her chapter on what publishers are looking for, different publishing houses and editors adhere to different style manuals, such as the *Chicago Manual of Style* and *New Oxford Style Manual*. Stacy Juba provides excellent advice for you in her chapter, and as you read through the book, you'll see that each author adheres to their chosen style guides.

Not only does this model there's room for everyone's personality and style, but it will give you a feel for them and the way they communicate.

My advice to you is to read Launch Pad: The Countdown to Writing Your Book one chapter at a time. Then re-read it. Next, go to the countdown at the end of each chapter and work your way through the ten points.

Each author has given you that top ten countdown as the literal launchpad for you to start, revise, and finish your novel. The advice contained within this book gives you the best possible start to your writing career. I urge you to take the time to read each chapter and do the work involved, because writing a novel *is* work. It's fun, yes, but it is also work. Work that will feed your soul, stimulate your creativity, and help you live a more fulfilled life.

Take it from me—writing a novel is not just about the words on the page but about who you become in the process.

Emma XX

Scotland, February 2023

Online Research Tools for Writers
Meredith R. Stoddard

We live in an interesting time when it comes to researching anything. We have libraries-worth of information at our fingertips, and yet it's hard to know which information we can trust. News agencies sometimes blur the lines between news, opinion, and advertising. Social media algorithms promote posts based on engagement, not accuracy, giving the most inflammatory information more attention and often drowning out more accurate or nuanced approaches. Crowdsourcing reference sites like Wikipedia mean that you don't always know if you can trust the information that is given. And search engines sometimes prioritize ads over actual results.

Of course, when we're writing and publishing, accuracy is important. Even fantasy writers like me need to make sure the worlds we build are believable. The smallest inaccuracies or improbabilities can disrupt a reader's suspension of disbelief. If you're writing with all five senses in mind, research can be about anything from the scenery, to weather, to the sounds and smells of your settings and how your characters react. While researching my books, I've learned everything from a new language to the workings of the emergency brake on a 1989 Honda Civic.

In this chapter, we will go over:

- Getting the most accurate search results
- Checking your sources
- Which sites will be the most useful
- Ways to go the extra mile and ensure accuracy before you publish

In this age of questionable sources, how do we find information, and how do we make sure what we find is as accurate as possible? Let's start with how to find the best information we can.

Smart Searching

First, let's talk about search engines and how they work. There are a number of search engines to choose from. However, most internet users are familiar with only the top two: Google and Bing. Either of these should give you the results that you are looking for. However, you'll probably notice that they often return ads and news articles at the top of your search results. Ads may even look like articles in the way they are displayed, but will have the word "Ad" in front. Google puts that in bold print. Bing puts it in gray print that isn't quite as noticeable. Scroll down to below the ads and you will probably see some related questions that other users have asked on the topic of your search, but you may need to scroll past them to see the results of your search.

With billions of websites and articles on the internet, and more being added by the day, the amount of information to be searched can be overwhelming. There are ways to maximize the accuracy of your search. Searching as specifically and accurately as possible will help narrow things down. You can use these tools with most search engines.

"" Quotation Marks: If your search terms include more than one word, and you want to search on that exact combination of words, then put quotation marks around them. Otherwise, the search may return results that include one or other of your terms, or both in a different order than you intended. For example: If you're looking for information about Washington Park, meaning a specific park, use quotation marks to narrow that search, i.e. *"Washington Park"*

- Dash: Use this if you want to exclude certain words from your search results. Let's say you want information on modern-day cowboys. When you search on cowboys, you get a lot of results about the Dallas Cowboys football team. You can exclude those football articles by using these search terms: *cowboys -football*

~ Tilde: If you want to include synonyms for your search terms in the search, you can do so by including a tilde in front of the word. For example, searching for *piano ~lessons* will also bring up results that include classes, coaching, and school.

Site: Did you know that you can tell your search engine to search a specific website for your terms? Using *site:* followed by the website you want to search will tell Google, or your preferred search engine, to search that particular site. For example: Reddit is a large internet forum. If you want to search Reddit for posts about Stephen King, you can use the parameters *Stephen King site:reddit.com*

| Pipe The straight vertical line or "pipe" will indicate an 'or' in your search terms. For example, *Netflix|Hulu* will get you results for Netflix OR Hulu. The pipe mark is on the same key as the backslash or left leaning slash on your keyboard. To type it, just hold the shift key and press that key.

.. Two Periods Two periods between two numbers will indicate a search within a numerical range. So, if you're looking for top songs from a certain range of years, you can search on *popular songs 1985..1989.*

Location: This will help you search for something in a particular location. For example, if you want to find botanical gardens in New York City, you would use the search terms *botanical garden location:newyorkcity*

Filetype: If you are searching for a particular file type such as a .pdf or a .gif, you can add the *filetype:pdf* to your search terms. Let's say you want a .pdf of an article for a class you are teaching. You can search by the article's title or author and file type such as *Stephen King filetype:pdf*

Combining these tools: You can also combine these tools to narrow your searches further. Such as *"How to write a book" filetype:pdf.* This should return results of .pdf files with that exact title.

Consider the Source

Once you have the search results you're looking for, how do you know that information is reliable? The internet is full of misinformation and opinion stated as fact. Sometimes the articles that you find may be very convincing at first read, but a deeper look might uncover bias, careless sourcing, or outright malintent. Here are a few tips to help you determine the quality of the information that you find.

. . .

Be skeptical – If something sounds too good to be true or fits a little too neatly into a commonly accepted narrative, you might want to check the sources and facts.

Go to the source – If you're reading a news or blog article, look for references to sources. Make sure that those sources can be verified and check them for bias, as well. Peer reviewed academic studies are the gold standard but aren't always available for every topic. News wire services such as Reuters and the Associated Press are scrupulous about their sourcing and can usually be trusted. Things get murkier once you are looking at blog articles. You may have to drill down to verify some of those sources.

Know the business model – The internet is chock full of seemingly free sources of information. However, nothing is ever really free. Some sites make their money by selling ads, some by collecting and selling the data of their visitors. Some news sites are owned by organizations pushing a particular political or social agenda. Even think tanks which sound like they should be reliable sources are often funded by political action committees. Whenever you find a new source that you are unfamiliar with, check the "About" page on their website to see where they get their funding and what their business model is. You can even use some of the search tips above to search for *"site x" ~bias*. This can help determine how reliable the site's information is. It can also help with characterization if you are writing a character with a similar bias.

Use multiple sources – This is a journalistic technique that requires corroboration from an independent source before publishing. Make sure those sources operate independently from each other.

Fact-checking websites – Thanks to the proliferation of misinformation on the internet, there are now a number of fact-checking websites that can help you verify stories that you might find while researching. Here are three of the top fact-checking sites.

- **Mediabiasfactcheck.com** – This site was founded in 2015 to rate the credibility and bias of media sources on the internet. It gets its funding from advertising, subscription sales, and reader donations.

- **Factcheck.org** – This site is managed by the Annenberg Public Policy Center at the University of Pennsylvania. It focuses mainly on politics and public policy. It gets its funding from user donations, grants from the Flora Family Foundation and the Annenberg Foundation. Normally, the limited sources of funding would be questionable, but Factcheck.org has a proven track record of objectivity and is very transparent on their website about their funding and their process for verifying information.

- **Snopes.com** – Snopes.com began in 1994 as a website for investigating hoaxes and urban legends. The internet offers a platform for that kind of folklore to proliferate, and Snopes has evolved over the years into a fact-checking site for all types of misinformation. They get their funding through ads and merchandise sales, membership subscriptions, and donations.

The Top 3 Sites for Writers

Now that we've learned how to be smart with our internet searches and think critically about what we find, let's look at three sites that are often helpful as starting points for research. These sites have a wealth of crowd-sourced information and experiences that can help you when writing.

Wikipedia

If you're anything like me, you were a curious child who could be swept away just browsing an encyclopedia. I can still remember my excitement one day when I was around eight-years-old and we received our set of World Book Encyclopedias at our house. Unfortunately, by the time I got to high school, many of those articles were out of date. The world changes so fast that it's difficult for reference publishers to keep up. This is why most encyclopedias are now available online. However, professionally researched encyclopedias like Britannica require a subscription.

Enter Wikipedia, a crowd-sourced, and crowd-funded encyclopedia that is updated almost constantly by anyone. That's right. Anyone who wants to can edit a Wikipedia article. So, it's wise to be cautious using it as a direct source. However, Wikipedia and its staff have some specific criteria for approving those edits and maintaining the site's integrity. Yes, in the past some pranksters and internet vandals have edited articles in ways that were biased or outright wrong. However, Wikipedia has gotten good at catching and correcting those types of mischief. Here is what Wikipedia says about their standards.

> *Anyone is allowed to add or edit text, references, images, and other media here. What is contributed is more important than who contributes it. To remain, the content must be free of copyright restrictions and libelous material about living people. It must conform with Wikipedia's policies, including being verifiable against a published reliable source. Editors' opinions, beliefs, and unreviewed research will not remain. Contributions cannot damage Wikipedia, as its software allows easy reversal of errors, and*

many experienced editors watch to ensure that edits are improvements.

It's that requirement that information be "verifiable against a published reliable source" that makes Wikipedia so useful when researching. The articles on Wikipedia can provide a good overview of whatever topic you are researching, and they often provide links to related articles within Wikipedia. What is most useful, however, is the source material.

At the bottom of every Wikipedia article is a section that lists its references. This is essentially a bibliography of the article's source material from everyone who has edited that article. You can use this information to verify what you've read and find more detailed information. Consider it an internet card catalog that can point you in the right direction to learn more.

YouTube

While Wikipedia may have source requirements and fact-checking, YouTube is far less curated. Anyone can make and upload videos about almost anything as long as it doesn't violate the terms of service. YouTube does very little policing of the content on the site. It relies on users to report violations of its terms or copyright violations. YouTube does offer a great way to hear from real people about the things you may be researching.

For us as writers, YouTube can be incredibly useful for all sorts of videos. Here are a few types of videos that you might find helpful:

- **Tutorials** – There is a tutorial video on YouTube for almost any task from applying makeup to appliance repair. Sometimes they are even done by professionals. If you or one of your characters need to learn how to do something, check YouTube for a tutorial.

- **Virtual tours** – If you're researching a setting that you can't visit yourself, someone may have posted a video tour of it. These are also great for getting people's reactions to a place; how crowded it might be, and what it sounds like.

- **Product reviews** – Product review videos are some of the most popular on YouTube. They can give you insights into the products being reviewed, but also into the perspectives of the reviewers and how consumers think.

- **Commentary** – Much like product reviews, video commentaries can give you a variety of perspectives on an issue, place, or piece of media. Everyone has an opinion, and a lot of people voice them on YouTube.

- **Reaction videos** – Another popular type of video is the reaction video. These get people's gut reactions to anything from music to food. Often these reaction videos cross generations and cultures. They can provide some interesting perspectives on how people view things that people from other generations or other cultures enjoy.

- **Atmospheric videos** – While nothing beats going to a setting in person, there are videos of places on YouTube that give you a glimpse of the sights and sounds of a place such as voices, accents, and the cadence of casual speech. The creators of these videos simply set up a camera to capture the atmosphere. Whether it's a city dock or a coffee shop, you can hear and see what it is like. This can be so valuable for capturing the setting. Side note: If you're a writer who enjoys working in cafés but can't, there are atmospheric videos that can give you the background noise of a café.

Google Earth/Street View

Several years ago, my husband and I were driving through the Scottish Highlands and arrived in Ullapool. When we reached a crossroads and to my husband's astonishment, I didn't hesitate to tell him which way to turn. I had never been there before and didn't bother to look at a map. But I had written a chase scene through the side streets of Ullapool for one of my books. I spent hours on Google Earth and Google Street View plotting out my character's route and had gotten very familiar with those streets. That's the beauty of these two Google products. If you can't travel to a setting, you can do a virtual walk around it with Google Street View.

You can access Google Earth and Street View by going to maps.-google.com. Enter the location that you want to view in the Search bar.

Google Earth

This is a great way to get a bird's-eye view of your setting. It's good to orient yourself and look at the terrain. Search for the location you are researching. Initially, this will show you a graphic map of the area.

1. Click on the Layers icon, which looks like two sheets of paper on top of one another, and select Satellite. If you don't see an option for Satellite, click the More button, and it should appear.
2. This will give you a satellite view. You can zoom in or out using the plus or minus signs. You can also click and drag to move your view around.

. . .

Google Street View

Google Street View allows you to see a street level view of almost anywhere in the world. Google sends Street View cars out with cameras recording three hundred sixty degrees around the car. With this tool, you can walk down almost any street. It's a terrific way to explore settings that you might not be able to travel to or to remind yourself of places that you haven't been to in a while.

1. When you want to go to Street View, you can click the button in the bottom right part of the screen that looks like a little yellow person.
2. Then click Street View on the bar that pops up.
3. On the satellite view, double click on the spot that you want to see. This will take your view down to street level as close to that spot as it can. Faint gray X's mark streets that you can move along. Your mouse pointer will turn into a circle with an arrow in it that points forward.
4. Point the arrow in the direction you want to go, and if there is an X in that direction, you can click and move that way.

I have used these tools to explore settings everywhere from the mountains of North Carolina to the south of France. When you combine these tools with tour videos posted on YouTube, you can get the best sense of a place possible without actually going there.

Going the Extra Mile

As we've seen, the internet offers incredible avenues for research. However, sometimes we need to take things a step further. Google Street View doesn't show you how a place sounds, smells, or feels. If your main character has a career that you've never done yourself, there may not be resources available online to tell you all the things you need to know about that job. If characters speak other languages and you want to include a little of that in your book, or if someone in your book is from another culture or has a condition with which you aren't familiar, you may want to talk to someone who speaks that language or is familiar with that condition. Sometimes, first-hand knowledge is essential.

How do you know if you need to go that extra step? It's going to depend on how significant that character, setting, or element is to your book. Weigh the importance of getting it right with the cost of gaining that first-hand knowledge. Sometimes it's just a matter of taking the time to find and talk with an expert. If that's the case, you should take the time. Remember, getting something wrong can take your reader right out of the story. If there is travel involved or a sensitivity reader to be paid, there will likely be an extra cost.

Ask an Expert

No matter how good your research is, it's not the same as walking in someone else's shoes. Careers take time and experience to build, more time than we as writers working on a project have. When we're writing a character with a particular career, or covering a subject that might take a lot of time to research, it's best to talk to an expert. The good news is that experts often like talking to people about their passions. Finding the right expert is often the toughest part. Here are some ideas for finding an expert.

- **Social Media** – Social media sites that let users create groups may have sub-groups for professions or subjects of interest. You can try asking these groups and their members the questions you might have. For example, Reddit has a subreddit *r/legaladvice* where people can ask legal questions. There are two possible benefits to this. You can get multiple perspectives on the answers to your questions or users can refer you to a more reliable source for answers.

- **Professional Organizations** – The expert you're looking for might be in a particular profession. Look for trade organizations or professional societies for that profession. They should be able to refer you to someone near you who can help or maybe let you 'ride along' with someone in the profession to see what their workday looks like.

- **Academic Sources** – Check with universities or departments within universities related to the subject that you're researching. Search for the best schools for that subject. Then ask to be referred to an expert on their faculty. You can also use *scholar.google.com* to find an academic resource.

- **Expert Referral Sites** – There are websites that operate as databases for journalists to find sources. HARO.com and ProfNet.com are online databases where journalists can search for experts.

Going There

I was researching Inverness Castle in Scotland for some scenes in my second novel. I spent hours on Google Earth, Street View, and YouTube looking at the area around the castle and watching video tours of Inverness. But there were things that I noticed when I went that none of those sources told me. Google Street View didn't capture how fast the river flows. No YouTube tour could tell me how crisp the air is in the early morning, or how colorful it is at sunset. And none of them told me that the riverbank in front of the castle is teeming with rabbits. These are the kind of details that lend credibility to what we write.

Make the most of your research travel by putting yourself in your character's shoes.

- **How do they eat?** Go to the grocery store and look around at what they sell that might be different. What time of day do they usually eat?
- **How do they get around?** Do people there use cars, bicycles, or public transportation? What kind of cars are most common? What are the drivers and the traffic like?
- **How do people talk to each other?** This isn't just a matter of accent or slang, but also of tone. If you've ever been to New York City, you might have noticed that New Yorkers talk to each other differently from the way they talk to people who are from out of town. Also the general tone of everyday conversations is different from Chicago, to New Orleans, to Edinburgh. Capturing those local idiosyncrasies in your location will lend your writing credibility.
- **All five senses** – Videos and Street View can help with the sights and sounds of a place, but there is more to describing it than that. Proximity to the ocean or a body of water, vegetation, industry, all these things affect the way a place smells or feels.
- **Topography** – Is it hilly or flat? Is it easily walkable? This can be important when your characters are getting around.
- **What is the vibe?** There is a different feel to a lot of cities. New York, Philadelphia, and Washington, DC are only within a few hundred miles of each other, but they all feel very different. The general attitudes of the people are different. This is the kind of thing that is hard to capture in a video, and often must be observed. But it can make a huge difference in the believability of your writing.

Translators

Does your story include characters that speak another language? If you want to include another language in your story that you don't speak, you should make the effort to use it accurately. Mistakes in language can take readers who might speak that other language out of the story. You might not have to go as far as I did and take classes in that other language, but you may want to check with a native speaker before going to print.

Yes, there are computerized translators on the internet like Google Translate. However, Google Translate does not always account for the differences in structure that some languages have. Also, most of us don't follow exact grammar rules when we're talking with each other. Dialogue will include colloquialisms that computer translators don't cover.

People are going to be your best resource for this. Much like finding other experts, you can start your translator search on social media. Look for groups where people speak the language and ask for help. If it's a common language, you should be able to find an answer or sometimes multiple answers quickly. However, before you hit publish, you might want to have it checked by a professional translator. Social media groups can usually give you the name of someone happy to do short translations. You can also search on freelance sites like Fiverr and Upwork. If you're having trouble finding someone, you can also go to local colleges and high school language departments, or professional organizations for translators such as the American Translators Association for a referral.

Sensitivity Readers

No matter how much research you do, or how empathetic you are, there is no match for lived experience. Anytime that you are writing about a character whose lived experience is different from yours, you should consider employing a sensitivity reader. These are a type of beta reader who read a book before publication. Issues of race, ethnicity, sexuality, gender identity, religion, mental health, and disability can be very sensitive topics for some readers. A sensitivity reader can help you make sure that you are not using language, stereotypes, or tropes that demonstrate bias, even unconscious bias that will be offensive or damaging to these readers.

You should look for a sensitivity reader with lived experience of the culture, or subculture that you are concerned about. Sensitivity readers are usually paid, although rates can vary widely. Paying a sensitivity reader is far less expensive than publishing a book then being forced to defend or even pull it from publication because a group of people have taken offense at some element within it. A sensitivity reader should provide in-text comments in your manuscript as well as a final report.

You can find sensitivity readers on freelance websites like Fiverr and Upwork. There are also services where you can connect with readers based on their experience, like writingdiversely.com.

Conclusion

The internet offers writers some wonderful opportunities to research and connect with experts easily. Search engines are powerful tools that put information right at our fingertips if we use them smartly. However, we have to think critically about the information we find. Verifying sources can mean the difference between a believable and accurate story, or distracting readers with inaccuracies or misinformation.

Three websites that you will want to get familiar with are Wikipedia, YouTube, and Google Earth and Street View. These will help you find good sources and put yourself in your character's shoes, as well as understanding how people feel about some things that relate to your story, or how characters might react to certain situations. They are a wealth of knowledge and experience that we writers can use to build our characters and stories.

Sometimes we need to go the extra mile, literally, to visit the setting in our stories. We may need to consult with experts or employ translators or sensitivity readers. There are resources online to help us do all of those things. Use the research that you collect to create authentic characters and settings and build believable stories.

Top 10 Research Tips for Writers

10. Put yourself in your character's shoes – What would they eat? Where would they shop? What kind of things catch their attention? What is their job like? All of these things need to be researched.

9. It's more than just the facts – We don't just need facts. We need to research how people feel about things and react to things and events. YouTube is a resource full of opinions and reactions that will help you explore this for your characters.

8. Use smart searching terms – Use commands and tricks for maximizing the accuracy of search engine results.

7. Check your sources – The internet is full of misinformation and opinions stated as facts. Think critically and check your sources.

6. Use Wikipedia as an online bibliography – Wikipedia can be a great way to find primary sources.

5. Research for all five senses – When we write, we write for all five senses. So, we should research for all five senses.

4. Get a bird's eye view of your settings – Google Earth can give you a high level view of your settings.

3. Walk through your settings – If you can't go to a setting, Google Street View can give you the next best thing. You can walk down almost any street virtually.

2. Ask an expert – If you want to take a deeper dive into a topic and online research isn't cutting it, don't hesitate to reach out to an expert. Professional organizations, universities, and websites like HARO.com and Profnet.com can help you find them.

1. Perception is everything – Whatever your intentions, be conscious of how others might perceive the creative choices that you make. They may show bias in ways that you aren't even aware of. Sensitivity readers can help prevent you from offending readers. You can find sensitivity readers on freelance sites and referral sites like writingdiversely.com.

Meet Meredith R. Stoddard

Meredith R. Stoddard writes folklore-inspired fiction from her writing shed in Virginia. She studied literature and folklore at the University of North Carolina at Chapel Hill before working as a corporate trainer and instructional designer. Her love of storytelling is inspired by years spent listening to stories at her grandmother's kitchen table. Her *Once & Future Series* is a contemporary fantasy that blends Celtic legends with modern life.

She is also the proprietor of *The Book Grower*, a book coaching consultancy that helps authors and aspiring authors establish creative and business processes to keep them productive.

Find out more about Meredith and her work at:

www.Meredithstoddard.com

www.thebookgrower.com

https://www.facebook.com/meredith.r.stoddard

The Power of Working with a Book Coach

Emma Dhesi

'Book coach' is a term that you may have seen around the internet and very possibly ignored because you're not sure how coaching relates to writing a novel.

Perhaps it feels like something only published authors use, not writers who are just starting out.

In this chapter I'm going to delve into a brief history of coaching generally, how it moved into the book world and why having a coach is a vital part of your study and growth as a writer - no matter what stage you're a - but particularly when you're starting out.

What is coaching?

According to the Institute of Coaching Studies, the word *coach* was first used to describe "a large kind of carriage", and in the UK we still use that word to describe a bus that carries you from one city to another.

The Institute goes on to explain that, in the 19th century, people used the term as a slang way to describe someone who *carries* a student through an exam. The word *coach* then evolved to describe someone who trains athletes, and with which we're most familiar today.

In turn, *coach* spread into the business world, helping entrepreneurs and employees develop their leadership and effectiveness skills, after which it rolled out into the psychology and personal development fields.

The Institute of Coaching Studies likens "coaching with the metaphor of taking a car journey together. The client is behind the wheel, while the coach is on the passenger seat. The client decides when to start the trip and the destination. As the co-pilot, the coach simply holds the map and invites the client to explore different roads and make stops along the way to enjoy the trip."

This is a great way to think about coaching when it comes to your novel. The story is yours. Nobody can take that away from you. The coach is there to guide your path and help you avoid the potholes.

The Association of Coaching uses this definition: "*A collaborative solution-focused, results-orientated and systematic process in which the coach facilitates the enhancement of work performance, life experience, self-directed learning and personal growth of the coachee.*"

Notice the emphasis on collaboration and solutions. The coach helps you maximise your skills and life experiences so you get the result you want.

If you're wondering what the difference is between a teacher and a coach, it's this: teaching is one-sided. The teacher gives you new information, something you didn't know before. You can ask questions of course, but it is not the collaborative relationship you build with your coach.

Coaching encourages a two-sided discussion. The coachee is responsible for their own growth and comes to their own realisation about a situation or experience - or, in our case, their story.

Why has book coaching evolved?

Book Coaching is a new field that has emerged out of necessity.

As traditional publication has coalesced and financial margins have become tighter, agents and editors don't have the time or money anymore to invest in new writers, coach them, or guide them in their writing.

I remember reading Diana Athill's biography *Stet*, in which she described the nurturing of a new young writer called VS Naipaul. Over many years and with strong guidance (and even stronger patience) she took him from young writer to literary giant.

With the amalgamation of the big publishing houses and subsequent financial pressures, there isn't room for the long-term nurture of debut or mid-list authors. Publishers only buy books that they feel confident will reach a wide audience and make a profit.

Agents are by default in the same boat. Agents are looking to pick up a nearly perfect product from the slush pile. They don't have the luxury of time or budget to coax a great story out of a writer who has potential.

Profit margins are too tight.

Just as the merging of the big publishing houses has created an open marketplace for formerly in-house editors (good news for indie authors!) so, too, has it created a gap in the market for experts and professionals to help aspiring writers finish a first draft (which eludes an estimated 93% of writers), revise and even publish or query their books.

This is wonderful news for writers because it's slowly but surely breaking down the misconception that novels are written by the author in a bubble of isolation.

Novels have always been a collaborative project, worked on in-house by the author, agent and publisher. The cooperative aspect of novel writing is not a new thing.

I interviewed Jennie Nash, author, coach and founder of *Author Accelerator* and she told me that previously "the only way to get a book published was through a traditional publisher. And the agents and editors would help the writer, nurture their books, nurture their career, nurture them as a writer... that coaching was baked into the process. And as publishing has sped up... the publishers are wanting books to be what I call Camera Ready, ready to go, as soon as they buy them. They're not spending the time helping and nurturing and teaching and growing that writer, and so on the traditional side, book coaching bubbled up to fill that gap that the publishers can no longer offer."

How does a coach differ from an editor?

Simply put, a coach works with you throughout the writing process.

An editor comes in at the end, once the draft is finished.

Your book coach is invested in you and your future, as much as the manuscript itself. They are an important part of your life for the duration you work together.

I meet with my clients twice a month and in our meetings we, of course, talk about the book, but our relationship is more than that. Our discourse includes personal worries, including health, employment, and childhood experiences, all of which influence their writing.

As Jennie Nash writes, your writing coach is "a mentor, advisor, or guide to help you learn and grow while mastering a complex undertaking."

An editor is concerned only with the novel. They review the manuscript, put a very comprehensive editorial letter together and discuss that, and that alone, with you on a 50 or 60 minute call. Without a doubt, you will have revisions to make, and you're left to make them alone. So, although you know what you need to do, you're left to figure out how to do it.

There are three main levels of editing you need to be aware of. Know, too, that editors specialise in one or the other, depending on their skill set:

Developmental Editing:

Also known as Content or Structural editing. This is the big-picture look at your manuscript. This edit focuses on structure, pacing, story flow, and character development.

Copy Editing:

Also known as Line editing. This edit focuses on grammar, spelling, consistency, and voice. It also looks at the flow of your paragraphs and sentences.

Proofreading:

A proofread is the opportunity for a fresh set of eyes to pick up any last remaining errors or typos.

What does a book coach do?

Writing a novel is a long-term and intellectual endeavour. It's hard work keeping all the moving parts in your head while at the same time maintaining perspective on the story as a whole.

If you've experienced coaching in any other part of your life, you know how beneficial the experience is.

Most writers come to a coach knowing the basics, at least in theory. They've attended classes, taken part in workshops, read many craft books and scoured the internet for a magic solution to novel writing. It's not a teacher they need, it's feedback.

• Feedback

A coach really comes into their own when it comes to brainstorming ideas, asking questions about the script at hand, and working through a character's goals and motivations.

In my own writing, I've often got stuck with a plot point, or can't work out how to get my protagonists out of (or into) trouble.

Because my coach knows the story and the characters, they are best placed to help me come up with ideas on how to solve that particular problem. Oh the wonderful a-ha! moments I've had with my coaches.

• Set A Deadline

This is a crucial part of writing a novel - yes, even your first! Otherwise, and I know this from bitter experience, you will be writing this book for years to come!

Your coach will set a deadline with you, either for when you need to finish the next set of pages, or for when you'll finish the whole draft!

This is important because you need to know there is an end date for this project. Writing a first draft takes up a lot of time and energy and if it feels like a never ending slog, you are going to be less and less inclined to do the work.

You want to know when you'll finish the part of the process so you can celebrate it and recalibrate before you go on to revise.

Setting a deadline is scary because it means you're making a promise to yourself you're not sure you can keep. Your coach, through skilled questioning and gentle guidance, can help you keep that promise.

• Moral Support

The most surprising thing I've discovered, however, is that the story itself is only part of the coaching. The other half is the support I offer my students and get from my own coaches.

There is always a moment (usually about halfway through the novel) in the process where my students doubt themselves and wonder if any of it's worthwhile and wouldn't it be better for everyone if they just gave it up? Indeed, I've had those moments myself.

My job then is to help reframe my student's state of mind. Their book is absolutely worth pursuing. That's why it keeps them up at night! Their story needs to be told. Frustration and self-doubt are a natural part of the process and, with experience, my students come to recognise their own roller coaster of emotions.

• Professional Transformation

You need a coach who facilitates your transformation from a confused and lonely writer to a clear-headed and supported author. Someone who is as invested in your manuscript as you are. Your coach will take the time to read and think about your work, comment on it, ask questions and ensure your novel has all the necessary components.

A novel is more than pretty words, it's about structure and forward momentum.

Your coach will guide you to write the best book you can by asking questions of the plot, the characters, and the writing itself. They will ask just the right questions to unstick your story.

Working with a coach helps you clarify exactly why your work matters, what you have to say about life through your fiction matters. Not just to you, but to your readers and perhaps even the world at large.

Working with a coach demonstrates to yourself that you mean business, that this is important to you and you take your work seriously.

It's been my experience that the transformation shows itself not only in your writing but in your wider life. You're a happier person because you're doing what lights you up and this ripples into your professional life, your family life, and even your future goals.

- **Personal Growth**

Writing your first novel changes you. You become a new person. Perhaps not to the outside world, but inside you know you are not the same individual who started that manuscript all those months ago.

Pushing through your own glass ceiling, breaking old patterns of thought and behaviour opens you up to new possibilities. Now you know you can write a novel, you wonder if you can write two? Or a series?

Once you know how to construct a well-told and believable story, you create space in your psyche to consider your next challenge. To improve your writing craft? Be a guest on a podcast? Attend a conference? Host a workshop?

Beyond the book, you turn up to life differently. When I finished my first novel, I was a happier, more confident spouse and parent. I'd lifted a huge metaphysical weight off my shoulders, and it allowed me to breathe easier and show up for others with more ease and grace.

It made me generous with other writers one step behind me because, whilst I understood their fear of putting pen to paper, I also knew the personal growth that awaited them. I determined early on that I wanted to help other new writers to experience the life-changing ripple effect of achieving something you thought was beyond you.

Working with a coach allows you to see the skills you already have, pursue your dream when it feels too difficult, and prepares you to stretch for your next goal.

Will they help me write a bestseller?

That is something nobody can guarantee - no agent, publisher, or book coach.

Your coach will help you write the best book you can at that moment in time, but they can't promise book sales.

If you're looking for a get-rich-quick scheme, this isn't it. Building a name and a back catalogue takes time.

Do coaches need a qualification?

No. It's not necessary to have a qualification to be a book coach, just as it's not necessary to have an MFA/MA to be an author.

That said, it is necessary to be a book lover and, ideally, a writer. It is definitely necessary to study Story and understand its many and varied dynamics.

A qualification can give you reassurance that your prospective coach has invested in themselves and their professional development, but it's not a prerequisite.

Do they need to be bestselling authors?

Being a bestselling author doesn't make a person a good coach, so don't base your decision on that alone.

There are a lot of good writers out there who haven't hit the bestseller list. (You may even be one of them!) That doesn't mean they don't have value to share.

Do coaches have their own speciality?

As the coaching profession is expanding, many coaches are niching down to work with particular writers and stories.

For example, I work with first-time novelists. Others work with writers three or four books down the line.

I work across genres, but others specialise in historical fiction or thrillers, literary or children's stories. Some work solely on non-fiction books or memoirs. Others work solely on the first draft with you, while still others will take you right through to the querying process.

Think about the stage you're in and what kind of coach will be of most benefit for you.

Do coaches have their own frameworks?

Children's author and poet, Kwame Alexander, talks about working with his coach:

> "for the next eight months... Redlined my manuscript, modelled what my poems should look like, challenged me to get inside the

mind and heart of my characters, gave me reading assignments, told me my crap was crap, praised my word choice, listened, read, laughed out loud and told me things about storytelling that I simply didn't know. I'd finished it, and it was very good."

Each coach has their own way of working and will have their own framework, taking you from initial idea and premise, to outline to finished draft and beyond.

For example, Jennie Nash has her *Blueprint For A Book*, Lisa Cron has her *Bare Bones Logistics*, Lisa Tener has her *Bring Your Book To Life* Program and Jas Rawlinson has her *Changemaker Author Intensive*.

Ask your prospective coach how they like to work and over what timeframe. Some work for a few weeks at a time. Others, like myself, work on a 12-month basis.

Be sure to ask so you understand what's expected of the relationship and how long it will initially last.

How do I choose the right coach?

It's all about relationships. The most important thing, I believe, is that you like the person you hire.

- **Trust is key**

You're going to have some in-depth conversations with them, so you want to feel safe to discuss almost anything with them. You'll be amazed at what emerges from the depths of your psyche when you're writing a novel, and it can leave you feeling vulnerable.

- **Do they understand your goals?**

Be sure they understand your goal and will give you actionable steps to achieve them. Ensure they'll provide constructive feedback (good or bad) to keep you growing.

This is another reason you like the person you work with. They might give you negative feedback and it's imperative you feel those comments come from a good place.

- **What do others say?**

Look for testimonials and if you don't see any on their website, ask for them. All coaches worth their salt will be happy to do this.

What qualities do I need as a coaching client?

- **Be coachable**

The first and most important quality is being 'coachable'.

There's no point hiring someone to work with you if you reject everything they say. You must be willing to listen to what they say and their reasons for saying it. After that, you must make up your own mind.

Defensiveness gets you nowhere!

- **Willing to try**

The second essential is that you are willing to try new things. Your coach may suggest new ways of writing or approaching your work, things you've not tried before.

Before you reject them, try them. You never know, it might just be the solution to your problem.

- **Committed**

The third quality you need is to be ready to write. You want to make the most of your time with your coach. Commit to the novel for the length of time you're with your coach and, together, set a deadline you know you can work to. Take advantage of their expertise and feedback.

A coach can do many things, but they cannot write your novel for you.

How do I know if I need a coach?

- **Going round in circles**

You've been writing the same story for over five years, and it's still not finished. You get so far, then give up because you don't think the story is any good.

What I've observed is that the story is fine and has real potential. What's missing are what the *Blueprint for a Novel* calls the "Story Fundamentals", such as why you're writing this story in the first place! Once you have those worked out your novel will get stronger.

- **No clear boundaries**

If you find it hard to set your own boundaries around your time and your priorities, you're probably what Gretchen Ruben calls an "Obliger." In her book *The Four Tendencies,* she outlines four main tendencies people display in their lives:

- Upholder - someone who follows through on both their expectations of themselves, and those others place on them.
- Obliger - someone who upholds others' expectations of them, but who can't keep their promises to themselves.
- Questioner - someone who will follow through on their own expectations of themselves, but will resist the expectations others put on them.
- Rebel - the person who resists both their own and others' expectations of them! (That's me, and can make life tricky!)

Ruben has discovered that "Obligers" are fabulous when it comes to doing things for other people, and would rather eat spiders than let someone down. That's all good and well, but those people are not so good at putting in boundaries for themselves and being accountable to their own desires and priorities.

A good example of this is someone who drops everything to help out their adult children, even though they're grown ups! If this feels familiar, a coach would be an excellent asset to your team because you wouldn't want to let them down, would you?

- **Can't get an agent**

You've written your first novel, you're super proud of it, and you've set as one of your goals "getting an agent." But you can't get one. You know the story is a good one but you can't quite understand why nobody is biting.

This is when you need more than an editor because the problems lie with the story itself, not the finer details. A good coach and full manuscript review is exactly what you need to whip the story into shape and increase your chances of landing your agent.

- **Camaraderie**

The value in this is underrated. It's all very well being part of a writing group or a critique group (and you will get great community from those places) but those writers are focused on their novel. They're likely going through the same issues and need the same level of help you do.

But having someone who is focused on your work, and your work only, is vital to your writerly wellbeing. A coach stops you feeling so isolated in your endeavour. Yes, only you can do the actual writing, but when you have someone who knows your story as well as you do right beside you, it takes away the fallacy you're on your own.

You don't need to be a lone wolf.

Where do I find a coach?

Google, of course, is the best place to start. Try searching "book coach" and your genre and see who comes up.

Alternatively, you can look on websites such as https://www.autho raccelerator.com/matchme service, which will match you with a coach who works in your genre. I've put together a Pinterest board for you at https://pin.it/412QrEE, with many of the coaches I've come across and who work with a wide variety of clients.

I hope this chapter has helped you discover the power of working with a coach - in any area of your life - to write and finish your novel.

My coach has helped me grow as a writer and develop a confidence in my writing I didn't have when I was working alone. I wouldn't be without a coach now.

I've seen, too, the difference I've made in the writing lives of my clients. Not only do they tell me how helpful the coaching is, but I see the shine in their eyes when they have a breakthrough or write their best bit of dialogue to date. Their confidence takes a boost which encourages them to come back to the page again and again.

> "To finish writing a novel, even a first draft, is such an achievement, and I feel much more confident and knowledgeable about my process of writing." - Client testimonial

Coaching will do the same for you if you're open to being helped and want to write a novel you're proud of.

Happy writing!

References

What Is Coaching? (https://coachingstudies.org/resources/articles/what-is-coaching)

What's the Difference Between Coaching and Teaching? - (https://city-skills.com/whats-the-difference-between-coaching-and-teaching)

Alexander, Kwame. "This is what I know" *Swallowed by a whale - How to survive the writing life*. Ed. Huw Lewis-Jones. London: The British Library, 2020.

Athill, Diana. "Stet." Granta, 2011.

https://jennienash.com/

Top 10 Countdown

10. Determine if you need a coach. If you've been writing the same story for five years or more, it's time to hire a coach. If you're going round in circles and can't figure out why the story isn't working, hire a coach. If you're getting multiple rejections from agents, hire a coach. It's time to get professional help.

9. Get on the mailing list of a few different coaches. This is how you get to know a potential coach. It's through their mailings and any social media they do that you'll get a feel for their personality and how they communicate. This will determine if they're a good fit for you. Perhaps you need someone who will hold your hand, maybe you need a straight-talker. Some authors like working with coaches who push their buttons, because that's when they do their best work!

8. Book a call with the one you like best. This is the opportunity to hear more about their services and how they work. Do you feel safe in their hands? Are you confident they can help you?

7. Ask them key questions. At the end of the call, get clarity on anything they've said. Make sure you understand what you can expect from them, and what they expect of you.

6. If it feels right, say yes. Jump in. Don't let your inner critic step up and, yet again, strip you of your dreams. If the price is of concern, most service providers offer a payment scheme. Some might even offer a scholarship.

5. Take full advantage of your coach's experience and expertise. Nobody else in your life is going to be as invested in your novel as you and your coach. Bring them your questions and concerns. Ask them about craft as well as how to manage any nerves you're feeling about your work. They are there to support you.

4. When working with a coach, consider their feedback before responding. It's easy to either get defensive and reject every bit of feedback, or crumple in a heap and wonder why you're even bothering! Don't do that. Instead, consider the comments as objectively as you can. I always have a day to feel all the feels, then go back and really take in my coach's comments. She's usually 100% spot on!

3. Do the work! Your coach will bring their A Game to the relationship, but they can't do the work for you. This is where you must take responsibility for your work, your creativity and, ultimately, your future success.

2. Reflect on your journey. When you've finished your novel, take a moment to reflect back on your time. Consider where you started and where you are now. How do you feel? Do you see the personal and professional growth you've been through?

1. Take what you've learnt and start your next book. This is just the beginning! You now have a new set of skills of which to take advantage. Take them and go for it!

Meet Emma Dhesi

Emma Dhesi is a book coach and author mentor who specialises in helping beginner authors write their first novel.

Through her 1:1 coaching, Emma guides first time novelists through story development, character evolution and provides written feedback on your work. She navigates them through the emotional rollercoaster of finishing their first novel.

For more hands-off help, Emma hosts the podcast *Turning Readers Into Writers* and offers weekly support via her Facebook Page.

Emma lives in Edinburgh, Scotland with her husband, 3 children and 3 cats.

Find out more about Emma and her work at:

www.emmadhesi.com

https://www.facebook.com/emmadhesiauthor

https://www.linkedin.com/in/emmadhesi/

Outlining a Novel for Plotters, Pantsers, and Puzzlers Alike

Lewis Jorstad

As a child, I loved the classic *Looney Tunes* cartoons. Watching Wile E. Coyote dash through the desert only to run face first into a steel wall (or a falling anvil) was hilarious to six-year-old me—which, now that I think of it, probably explains why I primarily write dark fantasy.

However, now that I'm a writer, I have a bit more sympathy for Mr. Coyote.

Writing a novel isn't that different from trying to catch the Road Runner. You'll be sprinting along, happily putting words on the page as your story unfolds in front of you, when suddenly an obstacle jumps in your way. Your mental image of your novel becomes mired in sludge, and you slam face first into a hard wall you don't know how to overcome.

Outlining your novels is the classic remedy for these walls, and for good reason. An outline is a simple document that catalogs key details about your novel, helping you unravel your story before you start writing (when it's easier to see the bigger picture). This lets you write better first drafts faster, while also planning your way around those pesky walls before they strike.

Of course, plenty of writers experiment with outlining to little success—perhaps that's why you're reading this in the first place. It's not uncommon for writers to test drive an outline, but still find themselves clawing their way over dozens of walls just like normal.

So what gives? How can outlining be such a useful writing tool, while also being so prone to failure?

Well, the real problem here is your writing style.

I don't mean your writing style itself, but rather how your outline interacts with that style. Not all writers are the same, and not all outlines should be either. Some writers thrive with in-depth, detailed outlines, while others do best with sparse maps that only explore the bare essentials. Either way, your outline should be an extension of your writing process, and thus of your writing style.

This might put you in a bit of a bind. If you aren't sure what type of outline is best for you, you obviously don't want to waste months or years on something that isn't working. You need to know what your writing style is so you can craft an outline (and a writing process in general) that helps you, rather than hinders you.

So, we'd better start by asking an important question: are you a plotter, a pantser, or a puzzler?

Plotters, Pantsers, and Puzzlers

Before we begin, let me define our terms:

Plotter:

Plotters, like the name suggests, are writers who prefer to plan their novels in advance. Before beginning their first draft, they'll plot out the key events of their story, dig into their cast of characters, and research details for their genre and world building. By the end, they'll usually have a detailed outline mapping out their novel.

Pantser:

In contrast, pantsers (named so because they "fly by the seat of their pants") are writers who prefer to discover their story as they go. Sometimes called "discovery writers" these authors will dive into writing with a basic idea of their story, and slowly piece that story together as they move through their draft. Typically, pantsers will have only a sparse outline or no outline at all.

Puzzler:

Finally, puzzlers are those who write key scenes as they come to them, often in no particular order. Then, they work backward, filling in the gaps as they slowly puzzle their novel together using what they learn while writing. This is usually an iterative process, meaning many puzzlers enjoy the flexibility of some kind of outline, which allows them to experiment with their story from a bird's-eye view. How in-depth this outline is depends on the writer.

If you've spent much time in the writing world, I imagine you're familiar with at least some of these terms. The debate between plotters and pantsers is constantly raging online, and it's rare not to run into it at least once—or into the plantsing camp, which is a hybrid of the two. Puzzlers, though, are more unusual. This is the less talked about middle child of the plotter/pantser debate, describing writers who jump from scene to scene as they slowly connect the dots of their story.

In all likelihood, you'll gravitate toward one of these camps pretty strongly, in which case you probably already know what type of writer you are. However, if you're less sure, here are some questions that are worth considering:

- Does the blank page make me anxious, or excited?
- Do I spend lots of time sketching out ideas before I write them?
- Do I typically work on my novels in pieces, or write from start to finish?
- Do I have lots of notes scattered around and need to collect them all in one place?
- Do most of my ideas come as I write, or as I daydream or research?
- Why am I interested in (or wary of) outlining in the first place?

Fortunately, no matter what type of writer you are, outlining is a valuable tool for your writing arsenal.

For plotters, a traditional, in-depth outline is the norm. This gives you time to think through your plot, characters, and pacing, and to get those details on paper before you even start your first draft. If you're a plotter, you'll find comfort and structure in a thorough outline, but you'll need to be careful not to outline forever. Eventually, you will need to start your first draft and put all your carefully laid plans into action.

In contrast, pantsers often balk at the idea of outlining. As a pantser, you want to discover your story as you write, but that discovery can also lead to a lot of difficult dead ends. In this case, creating a basic, skeletal outline gives you a chance to plan a few key milestones or facts about your story. This way, you still get to discover most of your novel as you write it, but you're less likely to fall off the path entirely or write yourself into a series of frustrating knots.

Finally, puzzlers exist somewhere in the middle.

For most puzzlers, you'll have a clear vision of parts of your story and a black hole for the rest. You might know a handful of scenes or characters, but not much else. Here, writing a brief outline of what you do know gives you space to start filling in the blanks—and, more importantly, to ensure you have the basics. One of the biggest dangers of being a puzzler (which I personally am), is creating a bunch of richly detailed scenes, only to have no idea how they string together into a functional novel. Outlining your story pushes you to double check that you have a solid foundation, so you can eventually fill in the blanks as you learn more.

No matter what type of writer you are, outlining is a useful part of the writing process—so long as you adapt it to your personal style:

Plotters:

Most plotters benefit from an in-depth, detailed outline. This gives you the confidence of knowing your story inside and out, and also gives you space to experiment with different options before committing them to your comparatively more "serious" first draft. If you're a plotter, don't be afraid to take a few weeks or even months to dial in your outline.

Pantsers:

For pantsers, the basics are all you need. This gives you enough signposts to work toward, while leaving plenty of room to discover your story as you go. As a bonus, this doesn't take much time either! A simple, one-page outline could take you as little as one day— meaning you can capture that spark of excitement and get to writing quickly. Either way, I encourage you to plan the basics in order to set yourself up for the smoothest first draft possible.

Puzzlers:

Lastly, puzzlers exist in something of a middle ground. For these writers, the key is outlining the basics and then jotting down additional notes for any scenes or major events that are clear in your mind. From there, you'll have a good foundation to start puzzling your novel together, and won't have to worry about forgetting where you started from—which, when your story is constantly in flux, is a very frustrating possibility.

The Pieces of a Successful Outline

Now, we've talked a lot about the different types of writers, but we haven't exactly dug into what a successful outline looks like.

As I alluded to before, an outline is simply a document where you gather the most important notes about your plot, characters, and story. This eventually transforms into a map of your novel, guiding you as you write and revise your drafts. This is also a great chance to work through tricky parts of your story, too. Rather than fumble through your first draft when it's harder to see the bigger picture, an outline gives you space to pull back, get a bird's-eye view, and think about your story more analytically.

Beyond that, though, outlines are largely personal.

Because your outline will differ depending on your writing style, there is no one size fits all here. However, there are some common components I encourage you to think about. Deep down, all stories are built on the same basic foundation: A character wants something, sets out to achieve that goal, faces conflicts and obstacles, and thus changes or creates change in the world around them.

This is something we can work with!

There are five components nearly all outlines share:

Premise:

The elevator pitch for your novel. This is a one to two sentence synopsis of the core ideas driving your story. This doesn't include names or specifics, but instead focuses on establishing who your protagonist is, what they want, the conflict they'll face, and the twist that will make their journey interesting. For example, the premise of the 1987 romantic drama *Dirty Dancing* is, "A young idealist volunteers to help a friend get an abortion in secret, knowing the woman will suffer if she doesn't. In the process, she falls in love with a man far outside her social class, forcing her to realize that her world isn't as just as she's been raised to believe."

Conflict:

Next, your novel will need some central conflict to drive both your plot and your protagonist's character development. This differs from the smaller, scene-specific conflicts your story will include, like getting lost on the way to work, getting in a fight, et cetera. Instead, your *core conflict* is the primary obstacle, challenge, or threat your characters will face in your story. Resolving it is the point of your plot. You want this core conflict to be as strong as possible, because it's what will form the central spine the rest of your story builds on.

Protagonist:

Without someone to react to (and struggle against) your core conflict, you don't have much of a story. Enter your protagonist! This is the central character of your novel, the one your readers will identify with the most, and the one uniquely positioned to resolve your core conflict in the finale. Writing compelling protagonists is a massive topic all on its own, but if there's one thing to consider when planning your novel's hero, it's motivation. Your protagonist needs some desire or goal that forces them to take action, thus putting them in the crosshairs of your novel's plot. Note that it is possible to have multiple protagonists in one novel.

Key Characters:

Alongside your protagonist, your novel will also include a variety of other characters, but there are three that stand out in particular: your antagonist, key ally, and mentor. Your antagonist will represent the forces working against your protagonist, meaning they'll typically be a villain (though they don't have to be strictly evil). From there, your key ally will be a source of support and encouragement for your hero, while the mentor will share the wisdom or resources they need to evolve as a character and survive their journey. When combined, these three characters form a good foundation to build the rest of your cast from. Much like the protagonist, they'll also need their own goals and desires pushing them to take action.

Story Summary:

Finally, most successful outlines also include a quick and dirty story summary. This is a chance for you to map out the basic shape of your plot in a few short paragraphs, covering key details like how your story starts, how your hero gets involved, and how your story will end. With that said, this is a "quick and dirty" summary for a reason. The goal of this summary is just to map out a rough picture of your plot, so you have something to orient yourself with as you write. This won't be perfect or polished by any means, though you can certainly take the time to refine your story summary if you so choose.

Of course, you can certainly expand your outline beyond these basics, too. This is where you can dig into specific details depending on your story, genre, writing goals, and writing style:

Character Profiles:

Beyond your protagonist and key characters, your novel will probably include a whole cast of interesting faces. If you like, you can take the time to create character profiles for each of these characters, covering who they are, their role in your story, their primary motivation, and other details like their identity, history, and personality.

Scene Timeline:

Akin to writing a draft zero, your scene timeline is a chance for you to plan out the major story beats of your novel before you write it. This involves sketching out the basic stages of your scenes and then knitting them together in chronological order so you can see how your plot unfolds. This is a great chance to check for holes, work through tricky sections, and plan your plot points. For some writers, this is also a much faster way to puzzle their novels together in shorthand, saving them time when they sit down to write their first draft.

World Building:

Depending on your genre, you may have a lot of important world-building details to juggle—though I would argue that world building is important no matter what you're writing. Either way, it can help to develop a short world-building "rulebook," which catalogs key details about your novel's cultures, locations, social norms, technology, magic, and belief systems. This way, you can plan for these constraints upfront, rather than get halfway through your draft, only to realize your Victorian London detective can't have a cellphone!

Research:

Similar to world building, you may also have research related to your novel. This is especially true for any kind of historical fiction, though you could also use research as inspiration for more fantastical genres too. Regardless, this research is often well worth including in your outline, so you have an easy way to reference it as you write.

Comp Titles:

Speaking of research, many writers like to do genre research, too. For this, you would browse through other successful novels in your genre and collect a list of comparable or "comp" titles—books like yours, similar in genre and target audience, for example. These titles can both help you understand the market for your book and generate ideas when you hit a wall in your story.

Inspiration:

Finally, I'm also a big fan of including key bits of inspiration in my outlines. For me, this usually takes shape as a handful of sketches and music that I feel capture the tone or mood of my novel. However, I know plenty of writers who include images of all of their characters, locations, creatures, and tech. Whether you go in-depth with this or stick to the basics, adding some inspiration to your outline can be a huge pick-me-up when you're feeling stuck later on.

The question now, of course, is how to choose which of these pieces to add to your outline.

As we already discussed, plotters will probably gravitate towards more rather than less. Your five basics will give you a good foundation for sure, but taking time to plan out the rest of your cast and world building will give you an even stronger grip on your story.

From there, scene timelines are where things get good. Though not a requirement, creating a scene timeline gives you a great chance to work through tricky parts of your story from a bird's-eye view. You can mix and match scenes, experiment with different story structures, and solidify your vision of your novel before ever starting your first draft—which, for a plotter, is a huge source of confidence.

Meanwhile, pantsers and puzzlers might prefer to stick to the basics.

If you fall into one of these two camps, I still strongly encourage you to create a brief outline covering your novel's premise, core conflict, protagonist, and basic plot. This is your chance to map out key milestones within your story, both to ensure your story will work, and to give yourself the tools and knowledge you need to overcome any walls you hit while writing.

Beyond these basics, though, the rest of your outline is up to you—so much so that your final outline might only be a single page! Or, if you decide to stretch it further with additional character profiles and world building, maybe a few pages.

This is one area where I recommend trusting your gut. Though it can be intimidating, your subconscious will gravitate towards the right option for you. Listen to your brain and body as you outline your novel, and when it says it's time to start writing, take its advice.

There is one tip I want to extend to puzzlers in particular, though.

In my experience, having a scene timeline is invaluable as a puzzler. Even if your scene timeline has massive holes, this gives you a chance to map out what you do know about your story. You can then organize those scenes in a rough timeline and start to get a feel for how you might fill in the blanks.

This is literally like assembling a puzzle. Though it's the butt of many jokes online, writing your scenes on index cards and shifting them into place as you puzzle through your story can be incredibly helpful. Whether you complete that timeline upfront or slowly fill it in as you write your first draft is up to you.

How to Start Your Outline

Of course, knowing what pieces your outline needs is different from creating your outline itself.

There are dozens of ways to build an outline. You could write it all by hand in a notebook, print out an outlining template to clip into a binder, or create a document on your computer. Personally, I'm a huge fan of Scrivener (to the point that I've built a whole Scrivener system I reuse over and over), while others use whiteboards or specific outlining software. I've even experimented with programs like Canva, specifically for the ability to shift scene cards on a digital whiteboard as I puzzle through my draft.

Unfortunately, this means there's no one right answer here.

The best thing you can do at this stage is to consider what type of experience you're looking for. For simple outlines, a single sheet of paper or a document on your computer is probably the fastest option. Or, if you're highly visual, whiteboards or larger notebooks might make sense to you, so you can mark up your outline and add images, sticky notes, or highlights as needed.

Either way, I recommend experimenting. Dive into one or two options, and see how they feel for a day. If they don't click with you, try something else until it feels right.

The key here is making your outline a safe space for you to experiment.

Writing a novel is an iterative process, meaning your outline is bound to grow and change—and it will probably be pretty messy early on, too. All of that is ok. This is simply a way for you to work through your story's bigger picture before getting into the weeds of your first draft.

This also means your first draft probably won't be identical to your outline. As you write, your ideas will expand and evolve, and your draft might deviate from your initial plan. This doesn't mean you're doing it wrong, or that your outline was a waste of time. Again, your outline is where you'll experiment with ideas and get a handle on your story. You (hopefully) wouldn't assume your first draft is trash just because your final draft looks different. Your first draft was one stage in your writing process, and an important one at that. The same principle applies to your outline.

Of course, this doesn't mean your outline is just there to gather dust either!

The best outlines are *living* documents, meaning they change as your story does. As you deepen your understanding of your novel, don't be afraid to add notes to your outline, update character profiles or scene timelines, and just generally keep everything up to date.

Typically, I recommend making these changes in the margins, so you keep an original copy of your outline while still recording anything important. This way, when it comes time to start on later drafts, you already have a solid map to work from.

When Are You Ready to Write?

Ultimately, the hardest part of the outlining process is knowing when you're done.

There's always the temptation to outline forever, because it shields you from the challenge of writing your first draft. For many (whether you're a plotter, pantser, or puzzler) outlining carries a lot less pressure than writing, and is thus a lot easier to commit to than the writing itself.

Still, if you want to finish your novel, eventually you need to shift from planning to writing. Depending on your personal style, this shift will happen at a few different times:

Plotter:

Once you have a solid grasp on your story, it's likely time to call your outline done. For plotters, this looks like a clear vision of your key plot points and world building, and at least a basic character profile for all of your major characters. If you're in this camp, now is a good time to review your outline for any last-minute problems, and then dive into writing.

Pantser:

As a pantser, you thrive when you discover your story as you write —meaning your finished outline will be pretty sparse. You want just enough to move forward with your first draft, while still having a solid foundation. Do you know who your protagonist will be? Do you have a strong core conflict? Do you know the basic trajectory of your plot? If so, your outline is probably ready to go!

Puzzler:

Lastly, puzzlers generally have longer outlines that focus on a few key building blocks. You'll still want to cover the basics but, beyond that, your outline will really depend on your strong suit. Plot-focused puzzlers may have a rough scene timeline, while character-focused ones might gravitate towards character profiles. Either way, when you can see the dots of your story connecting behind your eyelids, that's a good sign that it's time to call your outline done!

Basically, when you start to feel that itch to write, it's probably worth listening to.

Your outline doesn't need to be perfect—and neither does your first draft, for that matter. The best thing you can do is start writing while you're energized and excited about your novel, rather than when that warm glow fades.

In the end, this is simply your chance to tell yourself your story. It'll be messy and unfinished, but that's the beauty of it. A successful outline gives you room to grow, honors your natural writing style, and helps you navigate your first draft with confidence—hopefully dodging a few steel walls in the process.

So dive in and start writing! Your outline will be a valuable tool, but first you have to give yourself permission to use it.

Top Ten Countdown Tips

10. Understand your natural writing style, and honor that.

9. Get clear on your premise early in the writing process, or as early as you can.

8. Pick a strong core conflict to form your novel's backbone.

7. Get to know your protagonist and how they'll change throughout your story.

6. Summarize your basic plot, so you have something to refer to when you get stuck.

5. Expand your outline as needed (again, considering your natural writing style).

4. Don't be afraid to experiment with both your outline and your story itself.

3. Remind yourself regularly that your novel is worth writing.

. . .

2. Give your story (and outline) space to grow and evolve as you write.

1. Strike while your ideas are hot and your story feels exciting!

Meet Lewis Jorstad

Lewis Jorstad is an author, editor, and story craft nerd who helps up-and-coming writers hone their writing skills over at *The Novel Smithy*. When he isn't working on the next book in his *Writer's Craft* series, you can find him playing old Gameboy games and baking homemade bagels.

Find out more about Lewis and his work at:

www.thenovelsmithy.com

https://www.instagram.com/thenovelsmithy/

https://twitter.com/thenovelsmithy

Harness the Power of Selecting the Right Point-of-View

Carol Van Den Hende

How do authors craft fictional characters that feel as real as a family member or a friend? The illusion might come from believable details, like how the curly sprigs of great-Aunt Betsy's gray roots remind us of someone we know, how their mannerisms are described, or the insight that their behaviors unearth.

One of the most powerful tools in our author toolbox is point-of-view. When we appropriately choose who's telling the story—and from what vantage point—we start from structurally sound ground.

In this chapter, we'll define point-of-view (POV), review the three types of point-of-view (first person, second person, third person), share ways to choose the right one for your work, and cover the impact of writing in deep POV. We'll then summarize with the Top Ten POV Countdown tips!

Point-Of-View Defined

Point-of-view is simply the perspective from which a story is told. Whose mind are you inside as a reader? Similar to decisions about which tense to use, POV foundationally shapes your work.

There are two fundamental types of POVs that novelists must choose:

1. Do I want to write my book in first person, second person, or third person point-of-view?
2. Then, on a chapter-by-chapter or scene-by-scene level, who should be the point-of-view character?

One key tenet is that for each chapter or scene, there should be one point-of-view character. The reader will only be privy to the inner thoughts of that person. We'll see actions and surroundings from the point-of-view of that character (except in the special circumstance of using an omniscient narrator, which we'll cover under third person POV).

First Person POV

First person point-of-view tells the story from the perspective of one character. The character speaks directly to the reader, using "I" and "me" pronouns.

This can be a powerful way to engage readers, as it's an immersive way to share what the narrator is thinking, feeling, seeing, and experiencing. You're hearing the actual words of the narrator, or their unique "voice."

Here's an example:

> "In the late spring of 1995, just a few weeks after I'd turned twenty-eight, I got a letter from my friend Madison Roberts. I still thought of her as Madison Billings. I heard from Madison four or five times a year, updates on her life that were as foreign to me as reports from the moon, her existence the kind you only read about in magazines...I was working two cashier jobs at competing grocery stores, smoking weed in the attic of my mother's house..."

In these opening lines to Kevin R. Wilson's *Nothing to See Here*, you get a sense of the main character Lilian's youth, her viewpoints, and how Madison is an important person to her. (2019 © Ecco, an imprint of Harper Collins). As a reader, you're charmed by Lillian's honesty and drawn to learn more about how she became friends with someone whose life is "as foreign to me as reports from the moon."

YA (Young Adult) fiction often writes in first person POV (and present tense) to create a sense of immediacy, an apt antidote to fleeting teenaged attention spans.

For example, take a look at these opening lines from Nicola Yoon's *Everything, Everything*:

> "I've read many more books than you. It doesn't matter how many you've read. I've read more. Believe me. I've had the time. In my white room, against my white walls, on my glistening white book-shelves, book spines provide the only color. The books are all brand-new hardcovers—no germy, secondhand softcovers for me. They come from the Outside..."

Here, main character Madeleine describes her world conversationally—from the pristine white walls, to having an abundance of time. She intrigues us by capitalizing the "Outside" world as if it's a foreign land (which, as you read on, you'll learn that it is for Madeleine, since her illness keeps her indoors).

In both these cases, the entire novels are written in Lillian or Madeleine's first person point-of-view, and we get to know them intimately well. As we'll see shortly, another option is to have multiple first person point-of-view characters.

Second Person POV

Second person point-of-view is one in which the narrator speaks directly to the reader, using the pronoun "you." This is less commonly found in fiction (though you may be accustomed to seeing it in advertising copy and non-fiction books).

Perhaps the dearth of second person POV is because its limited use can make it feel awkward and unnatural. However, this isn't always the case!

For instance, Erin Morgenstern takes on the challenge and creates an intimate story by using second person point-of-view in bestselling novel *The Night Circus*:

> "What kind of circus is only open at night?" people ask. No one has a proper answer, yet as dusk approaches there is a substantial crowd of spectators gathering outside the gates.
>
> **You are amongst them, of course. Your curiosity got the better of you, as curiosity is wont to do. You stand in the fading light, the scarf around your neck pulled up against the chilly evening breeze, waiting to see for yourself exactly what kind of circus only opens once the sun sets.**
>
> The ticket booth clearly visible behind the gates is closed and barred. The tents are still, save for when they ripple ever so slightly

in the wind. The only movement within the circus is the clock that ticks by the passing minutes, if such a wonder of sculpture can even be called a clock.

The circus looks abandoned and empty. **But you think perhaps you can smell caramel wafting through the evening breeze, beneath the crisp scent of the autumn leaves.** A subtle sweetness at the edges of the cold.

Examine the bolded sentences, where "you" is used to draw the reader more deeply into the opening scene. The author pulls you in, first by connecting with you through the universal insight that humans are curious beings, and then by wrapping a scarf around your neck against the chill night air. As YA author Barbara Newman says, "Second person, when done well, can be brilliant. It has the hypnotic quality of suggestion."

Here is another example of second person point-of-view, excerpted from the novel *You Are the One* by Aja Gabel, published in 2020:

You're the one who stays behind when everyone else goes home. You're the one who sits at the bar and nurses a drink, hoping someone will come and keep you company. You're the one who's always alone, who doesn't have anyone to go home to.

But tonight, something is different. Tonight, you're not alone.

You feel a tap on your shoulder and turn to see a familiar face. It's your ex-girlfriend, the one you haven't seen in years. She's smiling at you, her eyes bright and kind.

'Hey,' she says, 'I saw you sitting here and thought I'd come over and say hi. How have you been?'

You're stunned. You never thought you'd see her again, let alone in this bar, in this city. You're not sure how to react, but you manage to stutter out a greeting and ask how she's been.

In this excerpt, the narrator is addressing the reader directly using the pronoun "you," creating a sense of immediacy and intimacy. This creates a feeling of being in the conversation yourself.

Once you become accustomed to the perspective and cadence, second person POV can work beautifully well.

Third Person POV

Third person point-of-view is told using the pronouns "he," "she," "it," and "they." This is the most common choice in fiction writing and probably the one you're familiar with from reading years of classics in school. English and American authors Jane Austen, Charles Dickens, Virginia Woolf, and Mark Twain all wrote in third person.

Besides being common practice, there's good reason for the prevalence of third person POV. Writing in third person allows the writer the flexibility to choose multiple points of view and perspectives for each chapter or scene. (In the next section, we'll discuss how authors can also accomplish this in first person POV).

There are two types of third person points of view:

- Close third person or limited POV
- Third person omniscient POV

Close Third Person Or Limited POV

"Limited" simply means that we're in one person's point-of-view at a time. This doesn't mean that your creativity or ability to convey a story is limited.

It's important to limit the POV to one at a time because once a reader is attuned to one character's mind, it can be jarring to suddenly introduce another character's POV. In craft parlance, we dub this "head hopping."

Head hopping is a sudden shift from one character's perspective to another's. This can confuse a reader, and a confused reader may decide that your book isn't for them.

Here's an example of an abrupt change from one protagonist, Billy, to another... let's call her Jean. Peruse the lines as if you're a reader: first, you're in Billy's point-of-view, so how can you all of a sudden understand what's in Jean's mind?

> With a start, Billy spotted the stolen purse, with its three distinctive claw strikes marring its leather surface, looped over the crook of Jean's elbow. *How would he confront her?*
>
> Jean caught his glance and leapt up out of her chair. She wasn't going to let him judge her. He couldn't possibly understand her motives. She clutched her dead sister's purse, ready to flee.

A better alternative would be to show Jean's emotion from Billy's vantage point:

> With a start, Billy spotted the stolen purse, with its three distinctive claw strikes marring its leather surface, looped over the crook of Jean's elbow. How would he confront her?
>
> But wait. Color swept from her neck up her cheeks. She started to rise from her chair. Billy opened his mouth to explain that he understood her hardship. He needed to reassure her before she could flee.

In this second excerpt, Billy notices the change in Jean's complexion. When she rises from the chair, Billy starts to speak, showing the reader that he understands her predicament.

There's an art to choosing which character should hold the point-of-view in any scene or chapter. One helpful rule of thumb is to choose the character that has more to lose, or something unexpected to learn.

If you're not sure which person to pick, try writing the same section from both points of view. What you learn may surprise you!

Third Person Omniscient POV

An omniscient POV employs an "all-knowing" narrator who sees everyone's perspectives in a story, so nothing is hidden from the reader. This POV hovers above all the characters and describes the action from a holistic vantage point. While this may create a feeling of distance between the characters and the reader, it also can provide an expansive view.

Lauren Groff employs third party omniscient POV in her beautiful novel, *Fates and Furies*, a National Book Finalist:

> The drizzle thickened to drops. They hurried across the last stretch of beach.

> [Suspend them there, in the mind's eye: skinny, young, coming through dark towards warmth, flying over cold sand and stone. We will return to them. For now, he's the one we can't look away from. He's the shining one.]

She sets the omniscient voice apart with the use of brackets. As a reader, this almost feels like a wink, a window into an insider's perspective.

Multiple POV Characters

In first and third person POV, there's the additional choice of which character is telling the story, for the full book, for a chapter, or even for a scene. Let's pause and look at an example of first person again, but told through multiple points of view.

The novel *Mad Honey* provides a compelling example. Jodi Picoult and Jennifer Finney Boylan write alternate chapters in Lily and Olivia's first person voices. (Though they each take a turn writing a chapter in the other character's POV, too!)

Here's middle-aged Olivia's opening:

> From the moment I knew I was having a baby, I wanted it to be a girl. I wandered the aisles of department stores, touching doll-size dresses and tiny sequined shoes. I pictured us with matching nail polish—me, who'd never had a manicure in my life. I imagined the day her fairy hair was long enough to capture in pigtails, her nose pressed to the glass of a school bus window; I saw her first crush, prom dress, heartbreak. Each vision was a bead on a rosary of future memories...

Contrast that with Lily's younger teen voice:

> From the moment my parents knew they were having a baby, my father wanted me to be a boy. Instead, he got a daughter: boyish in some ways, I guess, but not in the ways that would have mattered to him. Every day he took time to remind me of all the ways I'd disappointed him, not because of anything I'd done, but simply because of who I was.

An individual author can also create multiple first person POVs. If you choose this route, just be sure to have each character sound distinctive (which is important in third person POV as well).

More common is having multiple third person POV characters. For instance, Anthony Doerr introduces us to five characters in his epic novel *Cloud Cuckoo Land*: Konstance, Zeno, Seymour, Anna, and Omeir. They vary widely in time and place, age, gender, circumstances, and world views. The distinctions make it easy for the reader to keep each POV straight. Hear how three of them are introduced in third person POV:

Konstance:

> Konstance shuts her eyes, sees the writer descend into the dark of the tombs. Sees him study the strange chest in the torchlight. The diodes in the ceiling dim and the walls soften from white to amber and Sybil says, *It will be NoLight soon, Konstance.*

Zeno:

> He escorts fifth graders from the elementary school to the public library through curtains of falling snow. He is an octogenarian in a canvas coat; his boots are fastened with Velcro; cartoon penguins skate across his necktie. All day, joy has steadily inflated his chest, and now, this afternoon, at 4:30pm on a Thursday in February, watching the children run ahead down the sidewalk... the feeling threatens to capsize him.

Seymour:

> In a dream, Seymour walks beneath trees toward a cluster of white tents, but every time he takes a step forward, the trail twists and the tents recede, and a terrible confusion presses down on him. He wakes with a start.

> The dashboard says 4:42pm. How long did he sleep? Fifteen minutes. Twenty at most. Stupid. Careless. He has been in the car for more than four hours and his toes are numb and he has to pee.

Each of these characters lives within a different setting, holds a unique set of motivations, and speaks in a distinctive way. Notice how Konstance's thoughts are expressed with a poetic other-worldliness, while Zeno's sentences paint descriptive details, and Seymour's inner dialogue after he wakes is short and choppy, conjuring his rapid-fire state of mind. (As a side note, it's incredibly impressive when these seemingly disparate storylines converge!)

How To Choose POV

At this point, are you asking yourself how to choose which POV to use? Recall that we started this chapter with novelists' nearly universal goal to render characters as authentic as real people in our lives. Choosing the right POV can help us achieve that.

Think of characters you've found so compelling that they've deepened your empathy, or shown you a window into a new world. How did the author achieve that? The main question to ask is "who is the main character or protagonist of your story?" The POV of your story should most likely align with the character whose perspective is primary to the plot.

Your next question then is how do you help that character's story to be most effectively told. To do this, consider the tone and theme of your story. For instance, more intimate tales may call for first person point-of-view, while third person point-of-view can provide viewpoints from multiple characters.

In my novel *Goodbye, Orchid*, my main character Phoenix hides an enormous secret from his love, Orchid. I use multiple third person POVs to increase tension. The reader has a full view of what's happened from Phoenix's POV. Therefore, as Orchid grows increasingly confused by Phoenix's actions, the reader feels her emotion, is invested in the story, and keeps turning pages.

So, ask yourself... do you want one character's unique voice to come through with great intimacy? Perhaps first person will work well. Do you feel comfortable telling the story with the reader invoked on the page with the power of the word "you"? Then perhaps second person is the right point-of-view. Would you like to tell the story from multiple points of view or use the familiar he/she/they framing? If so, third person point-of-view may be the way you're leaning.

To summarize, here are some pros of writing in first person POV:

- The reader experiences the story through the eyes of the narrator, which can create a sense of intimacy and immediacy
- The narrator's voice and personality can really shine through
- It can be easier to show the thoughts and emotions of the narrator

And some cons of writing in first person POV:

- The reader only sees the story through the eyes of one character
- Or, if you choose multiple first person narrators in the same story, it can be confusing for the reader to switch between different voices

If you're considering second person point-of-view, consider these pros and cons of using this perspective.

Pros of writing in second person POV:

- The reader feels addressed directly, which can create a sense of immediacy, engagement and connection

Cons of writing in second person POV:

- It can be challenging to consistently write in the pronoun "you" and to think about the reader's perspective
- It can break the magic readers feel when they're lost in a story, as it may remind readers that they're separate from the book
- It's less common in fiction, which can be jarring and unfamiliar to readers

Overall, second person POV can be a powerful tool for engaging the reader and creating a sense of connection, but it can also be difficult to use effectively. It's important to consider whether this perspective will be appropriate for your story and whether you are comfortable writing in this style.

Pros of writing in third person POV:

- It allows the writer to show the thoughts and actions of multiple characters, which can give the reader a broader understanding of the story
- In third person omniscient, the POV can feel more objective, as the narrator is not a character in the story

Cons of writing in third person POV:

- It can be less immediate and intimate, as the reader is not experiencing the story through the eyes of one character

- In third person omniscient, it can be harder to show the thoughts and emotions of characters, since the omniscient narrator is not inside their heads

. . .

Ultimately, the choice of which POV to use will depend on the goals and needs of your story. It's important to consider how each POV will affect the way the reader experiences the story and to choose the one that will best serve your purposes. Earlier, we shared that first person POV can be popular in YA fiction, and third person has traditionally been most common in fiction overall.

In the end, there is no right or wrong. It can come down to a matter of personal preference. A particular POV may feel right for one book, and you may experiment with a different one for another. Hemingway famously wrote in first person until he published *For Whom the Bell Tolls* in third person.

Master authors even mix points-of-view, such as Lauren Groff's example above. Like the famous axiom "rules were made to be broken."

Deep POV

Think of fictional characters that have stayed with you long after the last page. Research has shown that readers' brains light up in the same areas as writers' brains when they're writing those scenes.

How do you achieve that brain-to-brain connection?

One powerful tool is "deep point-of-view." Let's explore how you can use deep POV to strengthen your connection with readers, keep pages turning, and dive deeper into your own work!

Deep POV immerses the reader in the thoughts, emotions, and experiences of a single character.

Consider these ways to deepen your readers' experience:

- Use internal dialogue to show the character's thoughts and emotions. This can be a powerful way to convey a character's inner world and motivations.
- Use sensory descriptions to help the reader experience the world through the character's senses. Different characters will pay attention to different objects or activities.
- Use physiological responses to convey emotion. Usually, feelings show up somewhere in your body. Nervousness may invoke sweat. Strong passion may warm your body. Shame may flame your cheeks. Try not to use cliché responses, and don't overuse the same tics or same body parts (some of the most common ones that get overused are eyes, lips, mouth).

A widely known piece of writing advice is "show don't tell." In the context of deep POV, this means that rather than explicitly stating "I think this" "I feel that," show the feelings through action, behavior, reaction, and what happens physiologically.

Here's an example from a scene between the protagonist and his overbearing boss from TJ Klune's *The House on the Cerulean Sea*:

> "The children like you."
>
> "I like them," he said. "I wouldn't do what I did if I didn't."
>
> "That's not always how it is with others like you." She cleared her throat. "Or rather, the other case workers."

He looked at the door longingly. He'd been so close to making his escape. Clutching his briefcase in front of him like a shield, he turned back around.

The master rose from her chair and walked around the desk. He took a step back, mostly out of habit.

The reader understands that the main character, Linus Baker, doesn't want to speak with his boss. Klune doesn't state this outright. Rather, he has Linus "look at the door longingly", think about "escape" and "clutch his briefcase like a shield". Then he "took a step back," and we understand that his desire to escape is a common feeling in his relationship with his boss, since his backing up is "mostly out of habit."

Have fun with deep POV—experiment with ways to help you see through the eyes of the character and try varying ways to express that.

POV Considerations In The Beginning, Middle, And End

Consider the use of POV to help with the beginning, middle, and end of your story.

BEGINNING

At the beginning of a story, writers have an opportunity to create a meaningful and emotional connection with readers. Readers want to care about the characters they're going to be spending hours with. Blake Snyder does a great job describing ways to do this in his book *Save the Cat*. He says to make the character feel relatable by putting them in danger or showing them doing something heroic.

Deep point-of-view has a role to play here. When readers understand the goals, motivation, and conflict behind a character's actions, they care more. You can get them inside the head of one person. Here's where it's important to remember: show don't tell. That is, rather than explicitly stating "I think this" "I feel that", show the reader through action, behavior, reaction, and what happens physiologically.

MIDDLE

In the muddy middle, deep POV can ratchet up tension. In the beginning, you've planted the seeds of the character's quirks, flaws, and motivations. Use those to show how they'd react to what's happening around them. You can even use the way they interact with objects to represent the emotion you're intending to evoke, a technique sometimes called "objective correlative."

For example, the protagonists in Gabrielle Zevin's novel *Tomorrow and Tomorrow and Tomorrow* meet in a hospital, after main character Sam permanently damages his foot. His injury is a major source of conflict between him and Sadie—again and again, they must overcome misunderstandings about each other's motives. In the middle of the novel, when the author introduces a broken dancer statue that Sadie notices outside of her new apartment complex, the reader finds the symbolism emotionally moving.

> Sadie left the office and walked home to Clowerina, who now seemed to be mocking her with his foot that wouldn't kick.

After hundreds of pages, we're deeply embedded in Sadie's point-of-view so we understand that she'd uniquely notice the dancer's frozen foot; it's a detail that echoes the relationship struggles she and Sam have faced during all their years together.

· · ·

END

In the denouement or ending of a story, you can use deep POV to show the character's changed mindset, new insights, and character growth. This will contribute to an emotionally-satisfying ending.

Whether you're at the beginning, middle, or end, if you feel stuck with writer's block, changing POV can be one technique to help. If you've written your plot into a corner or the story seems to lack momentum, you can try switching POV or seeing the story from the perspective of different characters. One of my editors taught me these techniques to move forward when you feel stuck:

- Switch the point-of-view (POV) and rewrite a scene from another character's POV
- Brainstorm a list of 10+ things that would most pain or delight your character at this point in the story

POV: Top Ten Countdown

We've covered a lot! Here are top ten insights when it comes to POV...Consider which of them most resonate with your work:

10. Choose first person POV when you want the reader to be deeply intimate with one or two characters, hearing directly from them.

9. Choose second person POV if you want to invite the reader explicitly on the page, calling them out with the pronoun "you."

8. Choose close third person or limited POV for a flexible approach that allows the reader to be inside the mind of one or multiple characters.

7. Choose third person omniscient POV if you'd like to give the reader a wide view of everything that's happening.

6. Once you choose a style of POV, just like tense, stick with it through the book (though, as with everything, there are exceptions!)

5. Don't "head hop"—that is, don't jump from one character's perspective to another without a break in scene or chapter.

4. Strive to write in deep POV to engage the reader, especially when the scene calls for being zoomed up close. Choose distinctive speech patterns, things that each protagonist pays attention to, or other traits to keep the POV character clear.

3. In the beginning of the story, use deep POV to reveal character goals, motivation, and conflict. In the middle, use deep POV to ratchet up tension. At the end, use deep POV to show the character's growth.

2. If you're stuck with writer's block, try writing the same scene from different points of view. You may even learn something new about your characters!

1. Feel free to experiment with different POVs to find the right one for your project or your preference.

Use these Top Ten Tips and soon you'll be an expert in harnessing POV to deepen your relationship with your readers!

Meet Carol Van Den Hende

Carol Van Den Hende is an award-winning author, a public speaker, and MBA with 20+ years' experience in marketing, strategy and insights. Plus, she works in chocolate (there's no 'sweeter' job!)

Her novels *Orchid Blooming* and *Goodbye, Orchid* series are inspired by wounded veterans and have won dozens of literary awards, including the American Fiction Award, IAN Outstanding Fiction First Novel Award, and Royal Dragonfly's for Cultural Diversity and Disability Awareness. Buzzfeed, Parade, and Travel+Leisure named Carol's books a most anticipated read. Glamour Magazine recommended her "modern, important take on the power of love."

She's keynoted and presented at conferences like Writer's Digest, IBPA, International Women's Writing Guild, Rutgers Writers' Conference, Novelists Inc, Sisters-in-Crime and Women Who Write. She's also a regular contributor to DIYMFA, where she pens the Author Marketing Toolkit column.

Carol's mission is unlocking optimism as a writer, speaker, strategist, board member and Climate Reality Leader. One secret to her good fortune? Her humorous husband and teenaged twins, who prove that love really does conquer all.

Find out more about Carol and her work at:

https://carolvandenhende.com/

https://www.facebook.com/carolvandenhende

https://www.instagram.com/carolvandenhende/

Building Successful Scene Structure

Joe Bunting

Scenes are the basic building blocks of all stories. If you want to write a great book, start by writing great scenes!

But how do you actually write great scenes, the kind that grab readers' attention, draws them into your characters' lives and the world you've created, and build up to the big moments you're working toward later on in the story?

Oh yeah, and what *is* a scene in the first place?

In this chapter, we're talking about scenes: what they are, the six elements in each one, and how to write (or edit) one. By the end, you'll know how to use this process to make your scenes better, or perhaps even to write your very first one.

We'll look at some of the main scene types you need for the various types of stories, and we'll also look at some scene examples so you can better understand how scenes work. Finally, we'll put it all together with a practice exercise.

My big breakthrough when it came to figuring out how to write scenes was when I was working on my memoir, *Crowdsourcing Paris*, which came out in 2019. Here I had all of these real life events that happened, some of which were exciting and some which were filled with normal, everyday life things. The problem was that I didn't know how to take those events and turn them into a story.

I didn't notice that though until after I had written my first draft and was reading through it.

"There are some good parts in this," I found myself thinking, "some parts where the writing feels alive and you really feel there in the moment. There are also some bad parts, where the writing just isn't working. But overall, it doesn't feel like a real book."

But *how* to make it feel like a real book, like all the books I read and loved? After all, who wants to write a book that doesn't feel like a book?

It took me over a year to figure it out. I learned from Robert McKee, from Shawn Coyne, and from so many other story structure gurus.

But then, it all started coming together when I went scene-by-scene, rewriting each one using the process outlined later in this chapter.

The book that didn't feel like a book all of a sudden started feeling, well, like a real book! This experience changed everything for me, from how I read scenes to how I coach other writers. I even wrote a book of my own about the process, called *The Write Structure*, which shares the approach I've since taught to more than 100,000 writers.

First, though, what is a scene? Here's a simple definition:

> A scene, in a story, is an event that occurs within a narrative that takes place during a specific time period and has a beginning and an end.

In other words, a scene is a story event, and as I mentioned, it is the foundation of every kind of narrative.

Scenes have different lengths, but they tend to be 500 to 2,500 words long. (George R.R. Martin sometimes writes scenes that are 10,000 words long, which could explain why he's struggling so much to finish his books.)

Every narrative form is different, but the average novel or film has fifty to seventy scenes. Short stories, on the other hand, might just have one scene.

For a section of narrative to be considered a scene, it must meet several criteria.

1. **A story event**. The scene must contain at least one story event.
2. **A change.** The goal for every scene is change. A character starts out believing one thing, feeling one way, or doing one thing, but by the end they're believing, feeling, or doing something else.
3. **One specific period of time**. Most scenes will be just a few minutes in one day. Some scenes may also contain flashbacks of other moments.
4. **(In film) One setting**. In film, a scene is by definition one setting. In novels, they can often take place in multiple setting, but I think it's good for novelists to keep this in mind to simplify your scenes.
5. **Contains the six elements of plot.** These elements are exposition, inciting incident, rising action, dilemma, climax, and denouement. Let's talk about each of these next.

For a scene to work, it must have those six elements of plot, but what are the elements? And why do they matter?

The 6 Elements of Plot: How They Work in Each Scene

The six elements of plot can almost be thought of as a checklist, a way of thinking through each phase of your scene so that it works, so that by the end something has changed in the scene.

Let's go through these six elements. These can feel abstract, so as we go let's look at a few examples so we can see how they work in stories. We'll use the climactic scene from the Disney film *Frozen*, the "meet cute" scene from *Titanic*, and the opening crime scene from *Harry Potter and the Goblet of Fire*.

Note, there may be spoilers in these examples, but these are some of the most popular films of all time, so I assume if you haven't seen them, you never will! Nevertheless, feel free to skip these sections if you'd like to avoid spoilers.

Here's a brief summary of each of the scenes, which we will expand upon as we go through the elements (you will likely be able to find each of these scenes on YouTube if you search for them):

- ***Frozen* scene:** Act of True Love. This is the climax of the film, the second to last scene, in which Princess Anna is about to freeze to death after earlier being struck in the heart by Princess Elsa's magic. If she doesn't experience an "act of true love," her body will become ice.
- ***Titanic* scene:** If You Jump, I Will Have to Jump, Too. After living a life she doesn't want for too long, Rose plans to jump off the back of the Titanic to end her life. But when Jack sees her, he attempts to convince her not to jump.
- ***Harry Potter and the Goblet of Fire*:** A Groundskeeper Killed. This is the opening scene of the film, in which the groundskeeper at a large, seemingly abandoned manor discovers Voldemort hiding there.

Now that we have our example scenes, let's take a look at the six elements of plot, starting with the exposition.

Element 1. Exposition

The exposition's role is to set the scene.

What does the reader need to know or be experiencing for them to get the full impact of the upcoming events?

Exposition, when used well, is usually brief, often just a few paragraphs, and should be focused more on action and description than on sharing information. The purpose is to ground the reader's experience.

As a writer you will likely answer questions like, Where are we? Who are we with? *When* are we, in relationship to other events in the story?

Here are our exposition examples:

- *Frozen* **scene:** Princess Anna is wandering through a blizzard, nearly frozen, searching for Christoff who can give her "true love's kiss" and save her life.
- *Titanic* **scene**: Rose stares into the water at the back of the ship contemplating jumping.
- *Harry Potter and the Goblet of Fire* **scene:** An old man, the groundskeeper, makes tea at night.

Keep in mind, the action from these scenes are continuations from previous scenes. Nothing has changed, yet. The exposition's role is to set the scene and then get to the inciting incident as soon as possible.

Element 2. Inciting Incident

The inciting incident is a new event that upsets the status quo and begins the scene's movement.

It can be something going wrong or something going really well, but whatever it is, it begins a series of complications in the lives of the characters, complications that increase the stakes and that can only be resolved through a choice.

The inciting incident appears early in the scene, often within the first five paragraphs. You still need to set the scene with exposition, but some scenes will begin with the first sentence as the inciting incident, and then the writer will backtrack into the exposition.

- *Frozen* **scene:** Prince Hans discovers Princess Elsa fleeing through the blizzard and begins to confront her.
- *Titanic* **scene**: Jack discovers Rose and says, "Don't do it."
- *Harry Potter and the Goblet of Fire* **scene:** A light goes on in the manor.

Notice how each of these are relatively small actions. However, they are the *first* small actions that begin a snowball that grows throughout the scene.

Element 3. Rising Action

You know that writing advice to put your characters up a tree, then throw rocks at them, and finally bring them down?

The rising action is the part of the scene where you throw rocks.

Your inciting incident begins the movement of the scene, but the rising action is where most of the action and conflict occurs. This will often be the largest section of your scene.

The main purpose of the rising action is to build the stakes toward the dilemma, so that the choice that your characters must make is as challenging as possible.

The stakes are essential. Your audience needs to know what's at risk here, so throughout the rising action, reveal what your characters find important—for example their lives, their relationship, or their identity—and show exactly how that thing is at risk.

Rising action examples:

- ***Frozen* scene:** Hans lies to Elsa, telling her that Anna is dead. This causes Elsa to break down with guilt and grief, which clears the storm. Christoff sees Anna and begins to run toward her, and Anna stumbles toward him as well, until she sees Hans pulling his sword to kill Elsa.
- ***Titanic* scene**: Rose tells Jack not to come closer. Jack explains that if she jumps, he'll have to jump in after, then describes how cold the water will be. "You're crazy," she says. "With all due respect miss, I'm not the one hanging off the back of a ship here." He reaches his hand out to help her back over the railing.
- ***Harry Potter and the Goblet of Fire* scene:** Grumbling about kids, the groundskeeper heads out to investigate the light that's gone on in the manor. He walks through the creepy garden, into the house, and up the stairs, when he hears voices, a man talking about murdering a boy. As he steps closer, a large snake slithers past him and into the room with the light. He freezes.

Notice just how much longer these descriptions are than the exposition and inciting incident. As you can see, this is a much larger section, a combination of events rather than a single moment. But they all build toward one thing: a dilemma.

Element 4. Dilemma

The dilemma is the heart of every scene and the essential element of all drama.

It's also the single most important element. If you can find your scenes' dilemmas, you will instantly write better scenes.

A dilemma is when a character is put into a situation where they're stuck and have to make a difficult choice with real consequences.

Fight or flight. Right or left. Jump or turn back.

These are simple choices, but they have dramatic consequences *if* you've set the scene well and built up the stakes.

Dilemmas usually occur right in the middle of your scene, but they sometimes come a little later, depending on the scene.

While occasionally a writer will fully spell out the choice, they are almost always implied and not shown. They might appear as a moment of indecision on the characters' face or not at all. And yet, they are the engine that drives the story forward.

They belong in *every* single scene in your story (yes, all fifty to seventy of them, if you're writing an average length film or novel).

Dilemma examples:

- *Frozen* **scene:** Anna looks to the left and sees Christoff running forward to save her, but to the right Hans is about to kill her sister. Should she go to Christoff, preserve her life, but watch her sister die, or should she save her sister but sacrifice her own life?
- *Titanic* **scene**: Should Rose jump and possibly lose her life, put Jack at risk, and be really, *really* cold or should she turn back, risk sliding back into the life she hates, and risk trusting Jack?

- ***Harry Potter and the Goblet of Fire* scene:** Should
  the groundskeeper stay and try to find out who this person is
  and risk being caught or should he turn and flee and risk the
  person getting away (and perhaps being caught anyway)?

As you can see, these are powerful choices with dramatic consequences for the characters.

When writing my own stories, I almost always think about what the
dilemma will be for that scene before I start writing. I will usually
outline them as a choice with the following formula:

> Should the character choose [Choice A] while risking
> [Consequence A] or should they choose [Choice B] while risking
> [Consequence B].

Then, my only job while writing that scene is to figure out how to get
the characters into the point where that dilemma will occur.

Element 5. Climax

The climax is the highest moment of action and conflict in a scene.
The climax's source is the dilemma, which immediately precedes it,
and it shows how the consequences and results of that choice play
out.

If the inciting incident begins the scene's movement, the rising action
picks up the scene's momentum, the dilemma raises the question of
"what would you do in this situation" for the reader, then the climax
consumes all of the built up dramatic energy in one, big crash.

At it's most basic, the climax begins with a choice but ends with
consequences of that choice.

Example climaxes:

- ***Frozen* scene:** Anna chooses to sacrifice herself and save her sister. She sprints to block Hans' sword and turns to ice just as his sword is coming down, which shatters against her icy hand. Elsa, realizing what has happened, embraces her sister crying and saying, "Anna no no," while the nobles, Christoff, Olaf, and Hans look on. But, moments later Anna begins to once thaw back to life, as she supplied her own "Act of True Love" by rescuing her sister. Elsa realizes that the key to her magic is love, and unfreezes the kingdom.
- ***Titanic* scene:** Rose chooses to trust Jack, taking his hand and turning to step back over the railing. But she slips and nearly falls overboard. Jack is holding her arm as she screams. "Listen, I won't let go," he says, while sailors come running. He pulls her back over the railing and they collapse onto the deck.
- ***Harry Potter and the Goblet of Fire* scene:** Voldemort observes (through magic?) that the groundskeeper is standing outside the door. They bring him in, and Voldemort casts a spell—"Avada Kedavra"—killing him instantly.

Do you see how these climaxes both rise directly out of the dilemma *and* manage to heighten the action and suspense from the previous elements?

For the *Titanic* scene it would have been easy for the writer to let Rose get over the railing with no further trouble, or for the *Harry Potter* scene, the groundskeeper could have gotten away fine.

Instead, the writer presses deeper into the drama, heightening the action of the scene.

Element 6. Denouement

The climax is the moment of highest action, but it isn't the *end* of your scene. The final element is the denouement, also called the resolution, when you reveal what the world looks like now after the previous events.

The denouement, like the exposition, can be quite short, often only a paragraph or three, but it allows the reader to catch their breaths and gives you a chance to set up the next scene.

- *Frozen* **scene:** The characters celebrate the end of the storm, Olaf gets his own snow flurry so he doesn't melt, and Anna punches Hans.
- *Titanic* **scene**: The sailors discover Jack and Rose collapsed on top of each other, and considering she had been screaming for help, it appears as though he was attempting to assault her.
- *Harry Potter and the Goblet of Fire* **scene:** The groundskeeper dies (which isn't shown, but is implied), and Harry wakes up from a dream with his scar hurting. Was the whole thing just a dream?

Again, notice how short those descriptions are compared to the rising action or climax. The denouement is short! But, you can also see, especially in the case of the *Titanic* and *Harry Potter* scenes, how it sets up the events of the following scene as well as the story as a whole.

Do These Elements ALWAYS Exist?

If you're wondering if these elements are really in every scene ever written, the answer is no.

These six elements only appear in scenes that work.

I didn't invent these elements. They've existed for thousands of years, from the time humans would sit around campfires sharing the stories of their hunt, the poisonous berries that nearly killed them, or when they left the tribe to find a mate.

They work because they come down to the basic question at the heart of all storytelling, "What would you do in this situation? What choice would you make?"

Fight or flight, right or left, do or die, run or hide, try or avoid, and so on. These are questions humanity has always faced from before time, and the stories that we tell each other allow us to enjoy and learn from the experiences of others, fictional characters included.

Don't believe me? Try it out by studying your favorite scenes to identify the elements, or better, by using this process in your own writing. And if you want to go deeper, check out my book *The Write Structure* (thewritestructure.com), where I delve further into the nuances of each element and how they work in the rest of your book.

3 Ways to Apply These Elements in Your Writing

Now that you know the six elements, you can put them to use in three ways to improve your storytelling.

1. Study Scenes Using the Six Elements of Plot

"Books are made from books," Cormac McCarthy says.

Writers must not only *read* other stories, they must *study* them, understanding how each sentence combines to make the entire scene and the book as a whole work.

Use the six elements of plot to break down scenes by other authors to see how they work and how you can apply those lessons to your own writing.

2. Audit and Rewrite Your Existing Scenes

Do your scenes have each of these six elements? Are you missing any of them? If so, rewrite those scenes to include them!

When I first started using these elements to rewrite my scenes, I was shocked at how much better they turned out. It made me realize where I had let up on the drama and how to heighten the stakes and action to improve the scene.

To do this, read your scene, and then outline the story event and six elements as they stand now. Here's how it might look for your scene:

> **Story Event:**
> Exposition:
> Inciting Incident:
> Rising Action:
> Dilemma:
> Climax:
> Denouement:

For the dilemma, make sure to use the formula explained earlier:

> Should the character choose [Choice A] while risking [Consequence A] or should they choose [Choice B] while risking [Consequence B].

Also, keep in mind that the rising action will more likely be a list rather than a single sentence.

3. Outline a Scene Before You Write

Finally, you can use these six elements to outline a new scene before you write it.

This process will vary depending whether you're more of a pantser or planner.

For me, I tend to be in the middle, and so when I'm working on a first draft, I rarely outline all six elements, since I'm not exactly sure how they'll end up.

Instead, focus on the story event, inciting incident, and dilemma. As long as you have those three, the rest of the elements are likely to take care of themselves.

You Can Write Great Scenes Every Time

I truly believe everyone can become a great writer, finish their books, and get published, *if* you practice writing deliberately. I believe this so much, I created a whole website and community around it called The Write Practice (thewritepractice.com).

But how do you practice writing deliberately? Two of the most important elements of deliberate practice are *theory* and *practice*.

It's good to learn the theory of how story structure works, to read books like this one, and to study the craft.

However, theory alone isn't enough if you want to accomplish your goals. You also have to put that theory to *practice*. You have to apply these ideas by finding the six elements in your favorite scenes, by auditing your existing scenes and rewriting them using the elements, and by outlining new scenes.

If you found this at all interesting, don't file it away in your mind. Instead, put it to use in your writing today.

If you do, you'll learn how to reliably craft a scene that works every time and write a great novel.

Read on for the top ten countdown to apply these ideas to your writing. In the meantime, though, good luck, and happy writing!

Top 10 Scene Structure Countdown

How do you use story structure to write a scene that works? Use this Top 10 Countdown list, based on The Write Structure plot framework, to learn how to use the six elements of plot to better understand and write your own scenes.

10. Start by choosing a scene to study from a favorite book or film.

9. Find the scene's exposition. Find the six elements of plot starting with the exposition. The exposition's role is introduce us to the setting and characters in the scene, and give us information we need to fully experience the following events.

8. Find the inciting incident. This is the first event, large or small, that upsets the status quo and begins the scene's action, which will all result in the climax of the scene. It will usually appear within the first five paragraphs. Some scenes may begin with the inciting incident before backtracking into the exposition.

7. Find the rising action/progressive complications. What events create complications for the characters, either good or bad, pushing them to make a choice?

6. Find the dilemma. The dilemma is a brief moment, sometimes implicit, where the character has to make choice between two good or two bad options. It's the heart of your scene and of drama itself, so don't miss it!

5. Find the climax. The climax results directly from the dilemma and is the highest moment of action in the scene.

4. Find the denouement. If the exposition is what normal looks like at the *start* of the scene, the denouement is the *new* normal after the scene (at least.

3. Now, outline your scene. Using these six elements, outline your next scene, one sentence per element.

2. Next, *write*! Write out your scene based on the outline. If things are a little different by the end, that's ok!

1. Finally, audit your scene. Do you have all the elements? Could any element be stronger?

Meet Joe Bunting

Joe Bunting is a WSJ Bestselling writer, dad, founder of The Write Practice, and author of *Crowdsourcing Paris*. He cries in every movie.

Find out more about Joe and his work at:

https://thewritepractice.com/

How to Develop Suspenseful Scenes That Hook Readers

Samantha Skal

As fiction writers, our eternal goal is to get "just one more page" out of a reader. We want them to read our books in one sitting because they can't tear themselves away. We want to take over their lives for the time we have them in our story, to be so magnetic with what our characters, real or imagined, are facing that readers find themselves at every available opportunity picking up our book to find out what happens. We want them to finish the book we've written feeling both satisfied and desperate for more.

So how do we do this?

Suspense

When I think of suspense in fiction, it takes the form of that sneaking, prickling sensation that someone is watching you. Or the tightness in your stomach that something isn't what you thought it was. It's a heightened heartbeat. A nervousness. An anticipation. It's a certainty that something is coming, and you don't know what it is or when it's going to appear.

It's a feeling you can't ignore.

This tension—this suspense—is what we're aiming for when we write fiction. It's the engine that keeps a story running and keeps the reader engaged.

And because our goal is to hook the reader on page one and not let them go until we decide to let them go at the end of the story, suspense is an absolutely crucial part of writing an engaging novel.

And it applies to every genre.

Before we get into how to develop suspense in every scene, let's talk about the different types of suspense:

Suspense can and does appear in many different forms, and it doesn't always take the form of something scary. For example:

- Romantic tension is filled with a "will they or won't they" suspense: will they kiss or not? Does that look mean what I think it means or not? Will we have our happily ever after or not?
- Emotional suspense could be about acceptance: will I get into this club/university/secret society or not? Will I get that promotion/job/client/house? Will I win or not?
- Scary suspense usually centers around survival: am I being hunted or not? Will I get out of this or not? Am I smart enough to outwit the person doing bad things or not?

The common thread all three types share is this: they're about overcoming an obstacle.

One of my favorite craft authors, Rachel Aaron (author of *2k to 10k: Writing Faster, Writing Better, and Writing More of What You Love*), has a wonderful way of thinking about obstacles. Read her book for the full breadth of her wonderful advice, but the gist is this: take your character and put them in a tree, then light that tree on fire. Her point, at least how I interpret it, is to escalate the obstacles in a story, always. Don't ever make it easy for your characters.

Story is about change. We don't pick up a story to read about (for example) beautiful, rich, perfect-life Kristin having a perfect day. She gets up, she gets her coffee, she goes to work, she comes home, and she goes to bed. Nothing unusual happens. She loves everything about her life and can think of nothing that would improve her lot.

This is boring, because we want tension of some kind. We want suspense. Stories where nothing happens—where no one makes any decisions, nothing changes, and the point of view (POV) character is perfectly content—aren't engaging because we don't know why we should care. We want to read stories where someone wants something they don't currently have, where they face something, and they have to make decisions—hopefully hard ones—about how to get through it. The suspense the reader feels is whether or not they'll achieve their ultimate goal.

With perfect-life Kristin, an example of a goal on the page is that Kristin goes to work, but now we know she wants a promotion. She has her perfect day, she gets some good feedback from her boss and it seems like the promotion might happen next week. We feel some tension, because we know what she wants.

But, while a set-up for a story that shows someone wanting something not yet achieved is good, it's not enough to keep a reader engaged for a whole novel, because seeing someone achieve their goal with no obstacles is boring, too. There might be some suspense with the question of whether or not Kristin will achieve her goal, but it's not as suspenseful as it could be if there were more problems (i.e. more obstacles) in her way as she moves through the story.

As readers, we want to wonder how Kristin is going to achieve her goals, given everything she has to overcome. For example, what if her coworker gets promoted instead of her, and she finds out her partner is dating that same coworker behind her back? We feel the tension Kristin feels when the possibility of her achieving her goals slips away. We wonder, as she does, how she'll get what she wants. We'll be in the valley of despair with her when all seems lost when her ex marries her coworker and takes over the company, and then triumph with her when she figures out that she never wanted this job to begin with, and the thing she actually wants is to run a winery in the countryside with two cats, acres of land, and a partner who adores her.

That rollercoaster is suspense.

So, how do we go about designing a suspenseful story?

Before we get into that, let's establish some assumptions about where you, the writer, are in the process of bringing your story to life.

> **Assumption 1:** You already have a good idea of who your protagonist is, where they are in time and space, and what the overall story question is. The story question is the question posed in the book jacket copy or pitch for the story about whether or not the protagonist (the main character) gets what they want. Crucial to the story question is the reader's understanding about why the protagonist wants that thing and what the consequences are if they don't get that thing.

> **Assumption 2:** You have a rough outline* of what happens scene by scene in your story. Perhaps you've written the entire manuscript; perhaps you haven't. But in both cases you're relatively clear on what happens in your story.

*Pantsers, I hear you, outlining doesn't work for you. But at a certain point in the novel-writing process, we need to be able to see our entire story all at once in order to figure out where we need to shore things up. If you abhor outlining, approach the ten suspense-building tools below after you've written your manuscript, and then make an as-is outline (a chapter by chapter summary) so you know what you have.

If either of these assumptions is striking fear in your heart, don't worry. I have an answer. There are many books from wonderful craft teachers that cover how to build a scene and what propels a story forward, but the one I recommend above all others is Jennie Nash's *Blueprint for a Book: Build Your Novel from the Inside Out*. Her advice walks through the process of story ideation through outlining an entire novel, including an absolutely stellar tool she invented called the Inside Outline. The Inside Outline allows you to see your entire story in three pages, including the protagonist's emotional arc (which is a key part of writing an engaging novel). I swear by the Inside Outline in my own writing and for my clients, both on the planning and revising sides of the process. Learn more at www. jennienash.com/fictionblueprint, which also includes a wonderful 10-Point Checklist for confirming your Inside Outline (and your story) are shining as brightly as possible. The below advice is designed to be used *after* you have a 10-point checked Inside Outline and have addressed all other major issues.

Now that you have an outline, here are ten tools in the suspense toolbox to use and consider for each scene to ensure that each is as suspenseful as it can be.

For our purposes, we're making the assumption that scenes and chapters are synonymous and are defined as chunks of story that move the story forward.

Clarity of (Scene) Goals and Fear

As discussed above, suspense in a scene comes at a root level from obstacles to the POV character's goals. But without a clear understanding of what the POV character's goals are in a scene, obstacles mean nothing. If Kristin's coworker gets promoted over her and we don't know that Kristin wanted that promotion, the impact of that obstacle is hugely lessened.

As such, we want to be clear what the POV character wants in each scene and how that scene-level goal ties into their greater goal: the story goal.

Along with making it clear what the scene-level goal is, we also want it to be crystal clear to the reader what happens if the POV character *doesn't* achieve their scene-level goal. In other words, we want to make it clear what the POV character is scared of happening if they don't get what they want. These fears are the POV character's stakes and are the bedrock for developing suspense.

Take a scene where you have three people. The first person has a knife and is walking toward the second person in the kitchen. A third person stands outside. There are onions on a cutting board and a bottle of wine open on the counter. With no further information, we might assume that the knife-wielder is up to no good and wants to hurt the second person. Or we might wonder if the knife-wielder is heading toward the second person to help them cut up the onions and the third person is taking a breather from the party. The first option is filled with suspense; the second is not (unless you count the micro suspense of whether or not someone will cry from the chemical warfare that is cut-up onions.)

However, we have a much more suspenseful scene if the reader understands that the knife-wielder is under the impression that the third person is a scary person intent on doing bad things and is now terrified for themselves and the second person. To achieve their scene goal (to save them both), the knife-wielder might have to do something unthinkable, like kill the third person.

Because we understand what the knife-wielder is scared of, we feel more tension and more suspense. We understand what their stakes are, and as such, we're more engaged with the story.

Clarity of Opposition

Similar to clarity of goals, we (the reader) want to be clear in every scene what the opposing force is, so that we understand what to be worried about regarding the POV character's goals. We want to wonder: will the obstacle prove too much for our POV character? Will the opposing force win? Do we know why the opposing force wants what they want? When the POV character's goals and the opposition's goals are contrary and known, it creates some great tension.

For example, in the three-person scene above with the knife-wielder, perhaps we've seen a POV scene from the third person outside earlier in the story and know that they are indeed there to take out the knife-wielder and person two. Because they're outwardly presenting themselves as a friend, and because the reader is clear that there are two opposing goals (the knife-wielder wants to stop person three from killing them, and person three wants to kill the other two), the suspense is heightened. There's no way we're putting the book down in that situation.

There are many ways to portray the force of opposition in a scene, but the key is making sure the reader is aware of it. Some ideas: through the POV character's assumptions and translation of the world around them, via another POV, via a found clue (a letter, a text, etc.), or via dialogue.

Character Agency and Action

Agency is a term that gets used a lot in story coaching and craft, and for good reason. Stories where we see a POV character reacting to a lot of things happening *to* them aren't as satisfying or suspenseful as those stories where we see that character making decisions and being active instead of reactive. Said in a different way, even if an obstacle is something out of the POV character's control, we don't want them to sit idly by and allow the world to wash over them. We want them to make decisions about that obstacle, even if they're the wrong decisions. If they're in a terrible situation when the story starts (they lost their promotion and their partner to the same person like Kristin), we're reading this story to find out what the POV character does about it. Perhaps Kristin decides to wallow for a week and feel sorry for herself, but during that time, we feel her anger and her sadness and all the other emotions, and then see her decide to ruin their wedding out of revenge. She doesn't just accept the status quo. She does something about it, even if her decision is ill-advised.

In other words, in every scene, not only do we want clarity on the scene-goal and to see the POV character encountering a force of opposition (an obstacle), we want to see them make a decision about what to do about that obstacle and then take an action. The decision-making process, when it's on the page, has the added bonus of the reader understanding why the POV character is making that decision, which more deeply engages the reader.

To continue our example, this decision-making doesn't necessarily mean that the knife-wielder launches themselves through the window at person three (although they could consider this and reject it), but they could make a decision to play it cool and keep the knife nearby while they figure out how to keep things from escalating. Decisions move the story forward, and when motive and significance is clear to the reader, they also increase suspense.

Ratcheting Tension and Avoiding Repetition

Repetition in story is like throwing water on the fire of suspense. Readers read stories for a varied experience. We don't want to see the same obstacle come up again and again. We want to see new, even more intense things get in the way of what the POV character wants.

For example, let's take a romance plotline. The story question is whether or not persons A and B will be together in the end, and because it's a romance, we know that they will. Therefore, the suspense is all in how much they must overcome to be together. Perhaps Obstacle 1 is that they hate each other and/or have conflicting goals (A wants to save the old inn; B wants to tear it down to build a housing development). Obstacle 2 is that they start developing feelings, but they can't admit them because they're publicly fighting and each wants the other to back down. Obstacle 3 is that B's ex shows up. Obstacle 4 is a rumor about A's intentions with the inn that B believes. Etcetera. Each obstacle builds on the previous obstacle and makes everything worse. This is ratcheting tension and builds suspense beautifully.

If, by contrast, the same obstacle persisted throughout (B's ex was preventing them from being together), the story would be far less suspenseful.

Believability

Because every subsequent scene pushes us closer toward answering the story question, keeping the story question top of mind for the reader is key for keeping suspense high. Even if that path is tumultuous, winding, and paved with bad decisions on the part of the POV character, if the reader is clear about *why* the current scene-level decision is important to the greater goal and the decisions are believable and logical, we remain engaged.

The key here is the concept of believability. Readers will allow themselves to be carried along with a POV character and buy into their logic if the thought process for how the POV character got from A to B is on the page. Readers struggle when we see only the end result with no inner thought about that decision-making process. If a POV character is making a logical leap, keep the suspense and engagement up by letting the reader into the process of how they decided what they did.

Interiority and Misdirection

One of the very best ways to increase suspense in a scene is to use interiority, or inner thought. Because we, the reader, see the story through the POV character's eyes, we're going to see and feel what they see and feel. If it is made clear via inner thought or dialogue that what's happening is Very Bad or Very Good, we'll feel those same things and be pulled along for the ride.

Inner thought also allows the reader to engage deeply with the POV character and feel more connected (and therefore more hooked) into the story. All of the above—obstacles and what they mean, ratcheting tension, logic around decision-making—is achieved through inner thought. The more the reader can see *why* someone is making the decisions they are (and what those decisions mean to them), the more suspense we feel, because we've seen the POV character worry about several different outcomes. We understand that if X happens, Y can't be achieved, and Y is crucial for conquering the story question. The more we know regarding what to worry about, the more suspense we feel, the deeper the connection we feel to the story, and the more likely we'll say to ourselves "just one more page."

Inner thought can also be used to great effect to manipulate the reader into thinking what we, the author, want them to think. If character A assumes something about character B, we, the reader, will also assume that thing. If that (incorrect) assumption causes character

A to take an action, all of a sudden we're careening toward a big twist in the story when they realize that what they assumed was entirely wrong. As long as the inner thought is on the page about *why* the assumption is being made, the suspense remains heightened.

For stories with multiple POVs (i.e. the story is told from the standpoint of two or more characters), keep in mind what *the reader* knows at any given point, as opposed to what the POV character knows. Because the reader sees what every POV character sees (and thinks), suspense can be also developed by using the reader's knowledge that (for example) POV character A knows who the killer is, and POV character B assumes it's someone else. When character A deliberately tries to mislead character B, the reader feels that tension.

Twists, Reveals, and Intentionality

Twists and reveals are more common in mystery, thriller, and suspense than in other genres, but they can be used to great effect in all stories. In order to use them effectively, we need to understand their definitions:

- A reveal is the answer to a question the reader is asking themselves about the story (that ideally we, the author, have caused them to ask because we've planned it that way).
- A twist is the answer to a question the reader did *not* think to ask. Twists are often a new way of looking at a "fact" in the story, usually when a character discovers that an assumption they made (and assumed was fact) is not the case at all, and they were completely wrong. The more incorrect the assumption was, the bigger the twist will feel to the reader, and the more suspense they'll feel.

The key with both twists and reveals is the set-up. Twists and reveals need to make logical sense to the reader from the standpoint of looking backward at what they've already read, *after* they learn what the twist was. We, as authors, want to avoid a twist that the reader finds illogical because we haven't given them enough information to figure it out themselves. Readers are smart, and they're constantly looking for clues and hints (on the page) as to what will happen. If a twist or reveal is presented in the story without logical back-up, the reader will feel cheated and unsatisfied.

The answer to laying the groundwork for believable twists and reveals is to be intentional about what we (as authors) disclose to the reader when, and how we have the POV characters interpret those clues. Red herrings are clues that the POV character is convinced will solve the case or solve their problems, but actually lead nowhere. Subtle clues are on the page, but the POV character ignores them (perhaps they see the clue but dismiss it for a logical reason they explain). I find that when designing twists and reveals (or adding them to an outline that doesn't currently have any), working backward is best. Figure out what the twist will be, and then decide what disclosures the reader absolutely needs to make sense of that twist once it appears. For reveals, look at the entire outline and decide with intention when that reveal can be used for the greatest suspenseful impact on the reader. Keep in mind that every reveal and twist is followed by a natural break in suspense as the POV character resets and regroups on how this new information affects their scene-and story-level goal.

In well-paced stories, this ebb and flow is intentional and is a key part of keeping the reader engaged. To fix pacing issues, look at your entire outline. Highlight in red any high-tension scenes. Highlight in blue any low-tension scenes. If there is a lot of blue in a row, consider adding a reveal or twist that changes everything to raise the suspense. If there's too much high-tension in a row, consider adding a reveal or twist to insert that natural "take a breath" moment.

Hanging Questions

Hanging questions are a tried-and-true way of keeping suspense up at the end of a scene because they work. Readers will turn the page to find out the answer if a question is posed by the POV character about what to do next, or the action is stopped mid-way by a chapter break, or there's a disclosure of information that changes what we (the reader) think we know about the POV character or the story.

This might sound like manipulation, because it is. Being intentional about where to end a scene in order to entice the reader to turn the page is an easy way to increase suspense.

Don't Give Away the End

While sentences like "it was the last time she would see him alive" feel like they might add suspense, in practice, they don't. This is because the reader now knows what's going to happen. While we (as the reader) might be interested in finding out how this person dies, the tension-filled impact of a character suddenly dying is lost. For example, let's say that the person in question is about to do something dangerous. Knowing that he doesn't make it removes all suspense from a scene that would otherwise be incredibly suspenseful, especially if the POV character is watching and alerts us to what she's most scared of: him dying.

Meet Genre Expectations

Reader satisfaction, along with reader engagement, is our primary goal when writing fiction. One of the biggest aspects of reader satisfaction is delivering to them what they expect from the genre of story they're reading. Writing romance? There had better be a happy ever after (HEA) ending where the two people either get married or decide to be together. Writing a mystery? That mystery had better be solved by the end, and the vast majority of the loose ends wrapped up (and if they're not wrapped up, the POV character mentions they're not wrapped and is okay with it.) Writing horror? The reader is signing up to be scared, so deliver those heart-pounding moments.

This is a part of the suspense toolkit because knowing well the genre expectations for the story we're writing is a key part of keeping suspense high. If a reader picks up a story thinking they're going to get a romance and instead they get a thriller about a happily partnered person defusing a bomb to save the world, they're not going to feel the suspense we (the author) so cleverly designed around the bomb. They're going to get increasingly frustrated as they move through the story because the romantic tension they sought with this story is entirely absent. Whether they finish the story or not, they leave feeling unsatisfied and unengaged. We don't want that. We want to deliver the kind of suspense and tension the reader expects from that genre, and give them the best possible version of our story that hits every genre-specific goal.

Additionally, understanding genre expectations means that we (the author) can play with those expectations to raise suspense. For example, while readers of mystery know that the crime will be solved by the end, the more obstacles we put in the way of the main character and the worse we make it for them, the more suspense the reader will feel when it looks like there's absolutely no possible way that the main character will win.

A Final Note: Beta Readers and Reader Clarity

How our story is received by others is a key part of functional suspense in a story. Often, as authors, something may be very clear in our heads but not be clear on the page. Beta readers are a valuable resource, especially for stories with multiple twists and reveals, because a reader can only experience those suspenseful moments once. Each subsequent read will be less impactful, because the beta reader knows what happens. As such, betas are a key part of the suspense toolkit, as they allow us to understand how our story is being received and if our carefully planned out clues, twists, reveals, and red herrings are landing the way we intended.

However, beta feedback should be taken with a grain of salt. All beta readers come with their own filters, and sharing our work with others can be nerve-wracking.

To combat this, use beta readers with intentionality and great care. Make sure to select betas that love the genre your story is written in. Give them guidelines on feedback. i.e., instead of asking them to "let me know what you think," give them specific things to report back on. I like to use these questions and ask them to note the page number for each:

- When did you stop reading because you weren't engaged? This tells us (the author) when we might need to work on pacing or clarity with what the POV characters are thinking/doing.
- When did you guess the twist(s)? If the beta readers are guessing a climactic or final twist too early, consider backing off on the reader disclosures.
- When were you confused? When beta readers are confused or "didn't get it," it's an opportunity for clarity on the page, usually through more interiority from the POV character to translate what's going on. Clarity increases suspense, because the more clearly the reader understands the story and sinks into it, the more suspense they'll feel.

All this said, while having outside feedback is key for understanding how our stories are received, it's important to remember that we don't need to listen to every ounce of feedback. We can decide if the feedback resonates with our vision for our story or not and decide to do something about it, or not.

Closing thoughts: Books in the bookstore did not spring forth in their final state from nowhere. The authors worked hard on those stories and they, too, had moments where they had to fix pacing or suspense issues, or figure out how to work in a twist, or add more interiority so the reader was clear on what was going on. Books in the bookstore also went through seventeen pairs of professional eyeballs.

My point in saying this is that comparing our first drafts to someone else's completed, published manuscript isn't helpful. Enjoy the journey, and if you find yourself stuck, consider hiring a book coach.

The advice in this section was influenced by some of my favorite and most revered craft advice writers. I highly recommend all three of these books:

- Jennie Nash: *Blueprint for a Book: Build Your Novel from the Inside Out*
- Rachel Aaron: *2k to 10k: Writing Faster, Writing Better, and Writing More of What You Love*
- Lisa Cron: *Story Genius: How to Use Brain Science to Go Beyond Outlining and Write a Riveting Novel (Before You Waste Three Years Writing 327 Pages That Go Nowhere)*

The 10-Point Suspense Toolkit for Developing Suspense in Scenes

10. Clarity of (Scene) Goals and Fear: Suspense is heightened when the reader is clear on what the POV character wants in each scene (and why they want it), and what they're most scared of happening.

9. Clarity of Opposition: Similar to clarity of goals, we (the reader) want to be clear in every scene what the opposing force is so that we understand what to be worried about.

8. Character Agency and Action: Decisions move the story forward, and when motive and significance are clear to the reader, they also increase suspense.

7. Ratcheting Tension and Avoiding Repetition: Repetition in a story is like throwing water on the fire of suspense. Instead of the same obstacle coming up again and again, we want to make it worse as the story moves forward.

6. Believability: If a POV character is making a logical leap, keep the suspense and engagement up by letting the reader into the process of how they decided what they did.

5. Interiority and Misdirection: One of the very best ways to increase suspense in a scene is to use interiority, or inner thought. Because we, the reader, see the story through the POV character's eyes, we're going to see and feel what they see and feel. If it is made clear via inner thought or dialogue that what's happening is Very Bad or Very Good, we'll feel those same things and be pulled along for the ride. The more we (the reader) are clear on what's going on, why it matters to the POV character, what they're scared of, and what stands in their way, the more suspense we feel.

4. Twists, Reveals, and Intentionality: While more common in thrillers and mysteries, twists and reveals are a key part of keeping suspense up across all genres. Being intentional about what we (as authors) disclose to the reader when and how we have the POV characters interpret those clues is key for keeping suspense high. Intentionality is key for building suspense. The more we (the author) are intentional about what we want the reader to feel and think at every turn, the more suspense the reader will feel.

3. Hanging Questions: Keep the reader guessing. Being intentional about where to end a scene in order to entice the reader to turn the page is an easy way to increase suspense.

2. Don't Give Away the End: While sentences like "it was the last time she would see him alive" feel like they might add suspense, in practice, they don't because the reader now knows what's going to happen.

1. Meet Genre Expectations: When readers get what they expect, the suspense we've so cleverly designed will be more impactful.

Meet Samantha Skal

A fan of true crime and mysteries of all kinds, Samantha Skal (she/her) is a book coach and author from the beautiful Pacific Northwest of the United States. She is proud to be an Author Accelerator Certified Fiction Book Coach who specializes in coaching thriller, mystery, and suspense authors from novel planning and twist brainstorming through agent pitching, and especially loves revision (and helping writers get out of revision hell and into revision bliss.)

As well as being a proud member and fan of International Thriller Writers (ITW), she is closely involved with PitchFest at Thrillerfest, ITW's annual conference. She is also a many-time volunteer mentor for the Women's Fiction Writers Association (WFWA), and a member of both Mystery Writers of America (MWA) and Sisters in Crime (SINC).

After ten years working in HR in tech startups, she is absolutely thrilled to have her most favorite things, writing and story craft, be her full-time job. On most weekends you can find her either on a well-maintained hiking trail with lots of flowers or kayaking on calm water. She is an enthusiast of homemade sourdough, cheese of all kinds, stories that keep her up at night, and good red wine.

Find out more about Samantha and her work at:

www.samanthaskal.com

https://www.facebook.com/authorsamanthaskal

https://www.instagram.com/authorsamanthaskal/

Countdown to Building an Engrossing World
Susanne Dunlap

World building—that's just for fantasy and Sci Fi, right?

Wrong.

No matter what genre you're writing, you have to place your characters in a world that feels real to your readers. All stories require some degree of world building, even those that take place in the present day. It's true, though, that the more unfamiliar or imagined the world of your story, the more world building you have to do—much of it before you write.

Why before? Because character motivations and plot points should be integrated with the world of your story, and if you haven't figured that out ahead of time, you'll be struggling halfway through. Your characters, the conflicts they face, and their arcs of change need to be not only believable within the world you've created, but should be specific to that world.

Of course, there is a difference in approach depending on your genre. In Sci Fi and Fantasy, you're inventing a world. In paranormal, you're inventing the rules of a world that is parallel to the real world. In historical and contemporary, you're researching and reinventing. Even so, the process is the same. What differs is the degree to which you need to make a reader aware of the environment in order for your story to make sense.

For instance, you don't need to establish that the atmosphere is composed mostly of oxygen if you're writing historical or contemporary fiction. That said, if your story takes place in nineteenth-century London, you do need to make your reader aware of the unhealthy atmosphere caused by burning dirty coal and how that made your characters feel—how it affected their actions and decisions.

A note for fantasy and sci-fi writers.

I can see you rubbing your hands with glee about getting stuck into your world building, creating maps and charts and genealogies and laws, etc. That's all well and good, but read on for tips on knowing how to get out of your world building jag and onto the page.

I'll start by offering some basic parameters for world building and then talk a little about how you integrate that world you've either invented or researched into your story—without overwhelming the reader—and finally, how backstory intersects with world building.

So buckle up and get ready to sink your teeth into everything it takes to do the world building your story requires.

Start Here: Know What is Meant by "World Building"

World building is simply the process of creating a believable environment for your characters and your story. Believable means believable within the context of your genre, and the world you create can vary greatly depending on what that is.

Why is believability important? One reason is because the world functions as a backdrop, and if you've established it well, it will either engross a reader to the point where they're not actively thinking about it or transport them so that they can imagine that world and enter into it right along with your characters.

Another reason is that the world itself affects your characters, your plot, and the point of your story. More on that below.

No matter the genre, your world has to have logic and rules that apply throughout your novel. The more unfamiliar the world your characters inhabit, the harder you have to work to make it real.

But believe it or not, the principles are the same whatever kind of world you're building.

Basic Principles of World Building

#1: Get Physical

To make a believable world in which your characters live and breathe (if breathing is something they do), you need to have a solid grasp on the physical aspects of that world. The difference is a matter of degrees. In a completely invented world, you have to decide what the reader will assume and make sure you define everything else. If your characters are essentially human in physical or psychological makeup, you can assume your readers will accept that.

If they're not human-like, then be very clear in your own head what their differences are, and make sure your reader understands them.

The essential physical characteristics to take into account depending on your genre are:

Invented Worlds

- Universe—where does your invented world exist in its cosmos? If you're writing paranormal, where is that parallel world exactly?
- Atmosphere—what do your characters breathe? How does that affect the rest of the physical world?
- Flora and fauna—what grows and lives there, and how does that factor into what characters eat, their aesthetic experience of their environment?
- Geography—are there mountains? Lakes? Oceans? Swamps? Does the geography have an impact on the political structures?
- Climate—stormy? Calm? Hot? Temperate? Deteriorating?
- Physics—is up still up? Is there gravity?
- If you're writing fantasy, what impact does this environment have on the magic you create? How dependent is the magic on the precise world you build?
- In paranormal, how do these physical aspects of your world affect the non-human or para-human entities (ghosts, werewolves, vampires, etc.).

Researched Worlds—Historical Fiction or Exotic Locales

- Flora and fauna—be sure you know what animals and plants were around during your historical period or that exist in your unfamiliar locale.
- Geography—same as for invented worlds, only you're doing the research to make sure you get it right!
- Climate—this may be obvious to you, but depending on where you're setting your story, it might need to be clarified,

especially if you're writing a near-future book about climate change, such as Julia Glass's *Vigil Harbor*.

#2: Go from the Outside In

It may be tempting to start inventing or researching your world by looking at the specifics of your story, i.e. your protagonist's needs/wants/situation. While this is vital to creating your plot and character arc, it's a little more complicated with world building.

Why? Because those outside, physical and socio-political characteristics are the map upon which the action/reaction/decision/consequence trajectories of your characters need to unfold.

Of course, you can approach this any way you want, but having many of the basic world building blocks in place before you start writing can help you avoid a significant rewrite when, say, you've given a peasant a horse to get from A to B but discover that no one in his class would own a horse, let alone ride one.

The elements to consider beyond the physical world are pretty much the same for both invented and researched worlds. These are:

- **Basic human characteristics**—This is more for science fiction and fantasy, and for paranormal beings, but some thought should be given to this if you're writing in prehistory, for instance.
- **Socio-political power structures**—What's the class structure? Who wields the power? Is the system rigid or flexible? Are there tribes, clans, family units?
- **Religion**—What is the dominant belief system? How important is it in the society you are creating?
- **Money**—Who has money, and what kind, if it even exists? This is a sticky one for historical fiction, figuring out not

only what currency was in use but its purchasing power at the time.

- **Commerce**—What goods are valued, and how do they change hands? How do products get from their source to the consumers?
- **Arts and crafts**—Is art valued in this society? Is there an artisan class?
- **Communication**—Language is obvious but also the conventions around communicating. Hand-shaking vs. bowing, for instance. In the eighteenth and nineteenth centuries, there were also symbolic ways of communicating through fans and flowers. For fantasy and science fiction, are you planning to invent a language? That's a huge undertaking, but it has been done. You'll find a great list of invented languages that are learnable here: https://www. britannica.com/list/6-fictional-languages-you-can-really-learn. But be warned: an invented language is a huge undertaking.
- **Technology**—In any environment and in any historical period, it's important to establish the technology available to your characters, how they use it, and what effect it has on the society as a whole. Is the technology a force for good or evil? To use an example of how this applies in historical fiction, in the nineteenth century, industrialization caused massive changes in how people lived—some good, some not so good.
- **Transportation**—How people move from one place to another is fundamental to the human condition and likely will be fundamental to any fantasy or futuristic world you create. If you're inventing this, make sure it fits in with the technology and environmental considerations of your world. If you're researching, make sure to notice which transportation is available to which social class.

The additional consideration for fantasy is the **role of magic**. Any magic you introduce has to have its own set of rules. The reader has to understand what's possible, who wields the magic, what its uses and abuses might be, and so on.

There are many good resources on the Web that can give you lists of world building subjects to cover. What is trickier, in my view, is balancing the world building with your story development and knowing how much of your world your reader needs to see on the page so they are fully immersed in it, but not engulfed. More about that below.

#3: Get Specific

By this, I don't mean get lost in the details, at least not at the beginning. I mean make sure your character motivations and conflicts are specific to the worlds in which they exist. And do so even though, as in the case of historical genre fiction, the tropes of the genre supersede its historical setting. Those readers aren't just looking for a story they love, they're looking to be immersed in an earlier time. A time where there were dance cards and arranged matches (romance), fingerprinting hadn't been invented (mystery), or the only ships on the sea were under sail power (adventure).

A good example of what I mean by *specific* is in Anthony Doerr's *Cloud Cuckoo Land,* a masterful novel spanning three timelines:

- The siege of Constantinople by the Ottomans in the fifteenth century
- A contemporary public library (pre-Covid)
- A hermetically sealed living bubble that houses a whole social complex in 2045.

While there is a common thread linking all three—Aristophanes' satirical play, *Cloud Cuckoo Land,* and the importance of preserving stories for future generations—Doerr manifests this theme and creates characters and conflicts that could only exist in each of the different timelines and environments.

Anthony Doerr's worlds in *Cloud Cuckoo Land*, timeline by timeline:

15th century Constantinople

Here, Doerr has to take into account literacy rates and their effect on the characters, the attitudes toward physical deformity (in this case a hare lip), and the arts of siege and warfare when gunpowder was first employed. He has to have a clear idea of how manuscripts were stored, what those who had the stewardship of those manuscripts would do to protect them, and so on. He also has to take into account what actions the inhabitants of the besieged city would take as it becomes clear their city walls will not protect them because of the Ottoman's new technology.

Religion, too, is important. Constantinople was a Greek Christian city at that time, and the Ottomans would usher in Islam.

And he manages to do all this by showing rather than telling, by seamlessly interweaving the historical with the drama of the story itself.

Present day pre-COVID

Naturally, in this timeline, he didn't have to do a lot of world building for the reader. But the character of the non-neurotypical youth who is obsessed with the protection of his environment could only believably occur in a contemporary or near contemporary story.

2045 Sealed Environment

In this instance, Doerr was free to invent the rules of his world. In every scene, it's evident that he's thought through the physical, psychological, and emotional consequences of this artificial environment. These considerations—protection and safety vs. isolation; limited freedom of movement and thought; the relationship of the family unit to the community as a whole; how food is produced and consumed—power the story and make the inevitable conclusion feel very real. At the end, we believe the protagonist would have acted exactly as she did and would have been empowered to break through the artificiality of the world because of her accumulated knowledge and powers of observation.

Once your world is clearly defined, what does your reader need to know?

Whenever the question of what a reader needs to know arises, I remember the first time I heard of the iceberg principle, in a workshop led by the wonderful Lynn Freed at the Bread Loaf Writers Conference in 2003. There's nothing new about it, but it was new to me then.

This principle is simply that, although the writer needs to know everything from the tip of an iceberg to the submerged bottom, everything that has an impact on the characters or the story, the reader only needs to know that small bit that sticks up above the level of the water.

The iceberg principle is simply a way of saying *avoid the dreaded info dump.*

In other words, just because you, the writer, have done the work to figure it all out, don't feel obliged to put it all on the page. Details and information that don't advance the plot or move your protagonist along her arc of change will simply bog down your manuscript.

I know. It's hard. Especially in historical fiction, where you've spent months—maybe even years—on research. But none of it is ever wasted! Your characters and their environment will feel real and cohesive because *you* know everything your reader doesn't. And don't forget the author's note or historical note. That's where you can show off your research chops if you want to without interrupting the narrative drive of your story.

That leaves the question of *how* you figure out exactly what your reader needs to know.

Here's a simple test that makes a good starting point:

> If you've included a bit of information about the world you've created or researched that you really want to include (because it's oh so awesome!) but are afraid it might be an info dump, take that bit out, and read the section without it. If the story works just fine when it's not there, if your characters' actions and decisions make sense without it, consider axing that info from the text. If you still don't know, have a trusted reader read the passage that doesn't have the information in it and ask them how it sits with them. If no questions arise from them, you probably have your answer about how necessary that deleted passage was.

A Word about Science Fiction: Two Schools of Thought and Different Styles

A fundamental question to ask when you embark on a book project is exactly who is your reader?

And after that, make some observations about the books you love to read. How do they build their worlds? How much detail is on the page?

The reason this matters is that there are two different approaches to world building in science fiction, sometimes referred to as **hard** and **soft** world building. There's no judgment about which is "better," they're just different and appeal to different kinds of readers.

Hard world building goes into a lot more detail. It digs in deep on the futuristic technology—the instrument panels, the molecular changes, the exact effects and uses of different weapons—for instance. This kind of science fiction is often based in real astrophysics. If you write this kind of science fiction, you'll spend more time on the page creating the world for the reader, who likely geeks out on imagining that futuristic technology. The story considerations are still paramount, but someone who loves this kind of fiction will persevere through a lot more world building.

Soft world building pares the descriptions and explanations down to what's really necessary to the story, leaving a lot to the imagination of the reader. A reader arguably has to work harder to enter into that imagined world, but the focus remains on the action and logic of the story itself. This might be your approach if your story takes place in a near future and has human or human-like characters.

Again, think about what you like to read and why. Read like a writer!

World Building and Backstory: A Potentially Slippery Slope

Almost without exception, the world you build for your story has to be in place before the action of the story starts. You need to have a clear sense of how the world came to be as it is if you're inventing it and what conditions were in place historically by the time your story begins.

The issue here is, just how much knowledge can you assume on the part of the reader? If you've invented a world, your reader won't know anything about it. But that doesn't mean you get to fill in the entire history before you get to the actual meat of your story. It's up to you to figure out how to thread in enough backstory so that the reader isn't disoriented but not so much that it overwhelms the action.

With historical fiction, it's safe to assume a little more knowledge on the part of your reader in many cases. If your story starts after the French Revolution, for instance, you can assume your reader has enough information at hand to get the context. Same with a story that revolves around the Tudor court. But there may be specific things you need to work in that relate to your story, facts or events that are not common knowledge.

This can be done either within the narrative itself or as a prologue (but beware of prologues—they are to be used very sparingly and for the right reasons). The example I can give is from Maggie O'Farrell's book, *The Wedding Portrait*. Before the story starts, she includes a brief—and chilling—historical note explaining that 15-year-old Lucrezia de' Medici left Florence to marry the Duke of Ferrara and died less than a year later, and that it was widely believed she'd been murdered by her husband. Knowing this at the outset adds a huge amount of tension to the entire narrative. But O'Farrell tells the reader all they need to know about this in three sentences.

Give Yourself the Best Tools for the Job

Over the years, I have found that a couple of specific tools help me keep everything in my researched world straight. These tools are flexible enough to work with any kind of world building project. Of course, if you're good with having folders, a word processor, and a spreadsheet, that's fine, too. But the tools below have some features that are particularly helpful for writers of science fiction, fantasy, and historical fiction.

Scrivener or another tool like it (Atticus, Quoll, etc.): What Scrivener does is let you collect all your material in one file. You can outline, draft, import research, make character sketches, and just about anything else you can think of. Your work lives in a single file, so you don't have to hunt through folders to find something. And you can drag things around—especially useful for revising a messy first draft. At the end, you can output your manuscript to Word.

Aeon Timeline: I don't know if there's another tool quite like this available. Suffice it to say, it's a program that allows you to create any kind of timeline with any attributes you want and with an astonishing level of detail. And it can also sync with Scrivener through clever use of metadata—but that's kind of advanced.

Neither of these tools is expensive or on a subscription model, and some of the Scrivener alternatives are free.

"Help! Get me off the world building merry-go-round!"

So, you've got your tools, you've set the parameters of your story, and you're stuck right in it, having a whale of a time creating or researching your world. It's so much fun, you could do this forever!

However, at some point you have to start writing. And knowing when to stop (or at least pause) and get your story written can be a problem in any of the genres that involve heavy world building. Unfortunately, there's no single answer to this, because every writer is different and has a different process that works for them.

Instead of saying, "Do this!" I'll present a few possible strategies:

- **Establish the exact parameters of your story before you start.**

  This is especially useful in historical fiction. You needn't become an expert in every aspect of the period or event or person you're writing about. Figure out the boundaries, and focus your research and your world building there. In fantasy and science fiction, the boundaries can help you figure out exactly what your reader needs to know at the beginning.

- **Prioritize.**

  This, too, involves doing some story work first of all. What are the most important aspects of your world to power your story, to get your protagonist started on their story arc and put flesh on their bones? Figure those out first, and then build your world around them.

- **Remember that all things can change.**

  While it's important to get the foundation of your world in place before you start, it's inevitable that in the drafting process, things will change and develop. That's fine! Embrace it! But then assess how those changes affect your world building, and what they may add to it. If you're writing along and you find that a particular piece of magic isn't fulfilling the role you thought it would, step back and rethink it. If you discover you need some bit of research you haven't done yet, stop and do it.

Above all, give yourself permission to get it wrong at first, to have to adjust, to revise and rewrite. It's part of the process. And ultimately, you'll discover and refine your own process.

Countdown Tips to Effective World Building

10. Know your genre

Be clear on what your reader will expect from the world you're creating, how much detail they demand, and what tropes you need to be mindful of in order to satisfy your reader.

9. Establish the boundaries of your story

Limits are a creative person's best friend. Limits can help you focus on a time, a place, or an event that will, in turn, help you structure your world building and avoid overwhelm.

8. Set the physical characteristics of your world

Get the big picture sorted out first—atmosphere, climate, physics, etc.

7. Set the social/political characteristics of your world

Construct or deconstruct the power structures, commerce, technology, and so on.

6. Decide what your protagonist's conflict is—and make it specific to your world

To really get your reader invested in the stakes, the conflict must be rooted in the world you create.

5. Figure out how much your reader needs to know

If you find yourself waxing on about some cool technology or historical fact, raise a red flag and give it the "need to know" test (see above).

4. Line up your tools

Legal pad and pencil, Word, Scrivener, Aeon Timeline—use what makes sense for you.

3. Start sketching out your story or outline

You won't know everything about the world you'll need to create until you have a grasp on the story as a whole. Some writers create a classic outline. Others use tools like the Pixar plot formula or the Inside Outline. Still others graph their stories, lay them out visually. Do whatever gives you the best grasp of the complete world of your story.

2. Modify, correct, tweak your world

Learn as you go, check against your genre expectations, change what needs to change in your world based on your sketch or outline.

1. Write!

Meet Susanne Dunlap

Susanne Dunlap is a historical novelist and Author Accelerator Certified Book Coach. Her love of history began in academia with a PhD in music history from Yale. She soon decided it was much more fun to spin stories based on the remarkable figures and times she discovered than to write peer-reviewed articles, and published her first historical novel with Touchstone Books of Simon and Schuster in 2005. She made the move into young adult fiction in 2010 and published four YA historical novels with Bloomsbury Children's.

In 2019, Susanne stumbled into the orbit of Jennie Nash, CEO of Author Accelerator, took both the fiction and the nonfiction courses and became certified in both. It turned out that helping writers write the best books they're capable of and realize their cherished dream of becoming an author was a role made for Susanne, as the many testimonials from her clients in both fiction and nonfiction attest.

Today, Susanne continues to write and has a thriving business as a book coach in Biddeford, Maine, and considers herself the most fortunate of people to have a life completely immersed in books and writing.

Find out more about Susanne and her work at:

https://www.susanne-dunlap.com/

https://www.facebook.com/SusanneDunlapAuthor/

https://www.instagram.com/susanne_dunlap/

Finding the Core of Your Character
Kat Caldwell

Story is not about plot. Story is about characters.

When we are engrossed in a story, it's because we're following the path the characters are taking. The plot is used to force the characters into making decisions that will produce the story of growth, or the lack of growth, that makes the story worth reading. In other words, while cowboy shootouts, alien invasion, inheriting a castle, or government conspiracies are all interesting, what connects us to the story is the main character(s) and how they deal with these plot points. Whether the character is an animal, an insect, or a human, it is their inner journey, what they learn about themselves, that engrosses us.

Developing a character is extremely important for good storytelling. In fact, I'd say it's even more important than developing an intricate and interesting plot. The story could be historical or futuristic, but what makes the story successful are the characters and what type of journey they are on.

The minute we find a character who is boring or who doesn't change, who is all too perfect or all too perfectly evil, is the minute we lose interest. When a reader closes a book, it isn't because they don't enjoy pretending they're in Paris during World War II or in a spaceship. They close the book because they cannot connect with the character. The reader wants to feel like they know the character, so the writer needs to answer character-driven questions such as:

- What drives her/him?
- What thought process leads them to the decisions they make?
- How do they react to jokes?
- How do they react to injustice?
- How do they react to the telephone interrupting them?
- What do they do for downtime?
- What makes them happy?
- What do they secretly wish their partner could see in them?
- Who do they love more than anyone else in the world?
- What are they afraid of?
- What happened in their childhood to make them the way they are?

Developing three-dimensional characters draws your readers to your writing far more than your plot. Developing *interesting* characters is about more than choosing if they are short-tempered or snobby or ditzy. Readers are looking for characters they can *relate to*. As much of society becomes more comfortable with emotions, feelings, or traumas, so too do the characters in your books. Modern characters are much quicker to let the reader into their emotional world than were classical characters. But whether you're writing in a very close first person point of view or a slightly farther away third person point of view, most modern readers are looking for characters who are just as complex as they are.

Before we get started, I want to say that I am not dictating whether you ask these questions before you start writing or after. Every writer is different. Some are discovery writers and some are plotters. I know quite a few book coaches would say, "Don't start writing yet because you'll end up throwing many of those pages away." Which is true. But it's also true that I can't stop you, a writer, from writing. And I don't want to be a hypocrite. There are many times I simply can't resist writing out scenes before I have the character fully defined!

Developing Character Personalities

This happened to me in 2022. I started the year extracting a character from a book I had already begun after realizing that I was writing too much backstory. I decided to write the man's story, then write the woman's story, therefore creating a duology. It sounded like a fun, engaging, and (I'm embarrassed to admit) *easy* thing to do. I had already written a few scenes with the character, Tristen, so it wouldn't be too hard to create his story from thin air, would it?

Oh, yes. Yes, it would. I had some backstory on him, but the first book was focused mostly on Scarlett, which meant Tristen wasn't as fully developed. Not enough to write a compelling novel. Not yet. By placing Tristen as the only protagonist of a novel, I had to create a deeper and fuller character arc.

The first problem came up in March when I realized Tristen didn't have much personality. He was boring. One difficulty in developing Tristen is that he is a pushover and a victim of thinking he'll get people's approval if he goes above and beyond for them. The trap is a personality-less character or a whiner. Neither of which makes for a very nice read.

(As we continue forward, I'm going to assume you know the surface layer points of your character such as their age, gender, basic looks, etc. These are important, but external only. So, let's go a little deeper now!)

Finding a Personality Type for Your Character

There are five categories to choose from:

- **Openness -** whether they like to experience new things or stay in the comfortable. The opposite would be closedminded. This can also extend into curiosity and creativity,
- **Conscientiousness** - how much they plan, are organized and control their impulses. Those high in conscientiousness will work within the rules and delay gratification, those low in conscientiousness will be disordered and possibly impulsive.
- **Extroversion -** how outgoing a person is, how much they like spending time with other people and being social. Extroverts draw energy from being with people and introverts (the opposite) draw energy from being alone.
- **Agreeableness -** how a person reacts to those around them, whether sympathetic or helpful or not caring at all and more selfish.
- **Neuroticism -** how much a person worries, is vulnerable or temperamental. This has to do with someone's emotional stability.

You can find out more specifics about personality traits online. One option is to take a freely available test such as https://www.16person alities.com/from the point of view of your character to get more of a grasp on their traits.

If you prefer Enneagrams, you can find one at https://enneagramuni verse.com/. I'm not as well versed in them, but in essence, these different tests are basically trying to codify personality.

While I was taking the test, I had to think about how my character was going to react during the scenes that I had thought out for him. In the beginning, he came out as an adventurer, which threw up some warning bells in my head, but I went with it and continued writing. By the time I was halfway, I knew for a fact that he wasn't an adventurer. I took the test again, this time fully in his shoes, and he came out as an architect who leans to the turbulent, meaning he is emotional. And while my character has learned how not to show his emotions, inside he is emotional. This was the right assessment and the one I used going forward. This goes to show that characters can change as we write deeper into the story. I didn't have a full grasp of Tristen before I started writing, and you don't have to either. It's okay to get a few scenes in, or many scenes in, before taking a personality test for your characters.

Another point we have to look at when honing our characters is genre. Now that we have their personality, we need to work out what genre will let that personality shine.

The Question of Genre

Understanding what kind of genre you are writing is important when developing your characters because every genre has its tropes. While detectives in mysteries will each have their own flaws, they will also be a certain type of person because they represent the sort of humans who usually take those jobs. You can't have a squeamish detective who faints at the sight of a cadaver (unless there is a distinct reason for it in the storyline).

Let's take the character Elle from *Legally Blonde*. Her character is for a rom-com, so already we know she isn't going to become a detective or cop in a dark mystery or thriller. She's too peppy and Pollyanna. One of her flaws is that she sees good in everyone and expects everyone else to do the same. The writers made her a lawyer who could keep her big heart while still developing as a person.

In women's fiction, you need characters who are open with their feelings. This goes with family life fiction and sibling fiction. Romance is another that the reader wants thoughts and emotions from the characters.

This genre-character discussion isn't just for adult books, either. Even when developing characters for children and Young Adult novels, they should be deeper than the external level. YA may be for readers aged between 12 and 18 years old, but you still need to be aware of the reader's expectations of this genre to know how much of your character you're going to show.

Flat Character Arc

Successful books have dynamic characters, meaning that the reader watches them change and grow throughout the story. But there are some books with static characters. In these stories, the character *learns* something about the world around them instead of changing their view of it. **If you choose to do this, do it with purpose.**

Understand that even static characters still have to have internal and external conflict. Creating a non-changing character by accident is what we're trying to avoid. I advocate authors making decisions on purpose as much as possible. While sometimes readers will see things we didn't see in our story, I've noticed that when we receive a critique on something we did "accidentally," we tend to take the mistake to heart and beat ourselves up over it. Instead, if we have made decisions about our characters on purpose, we have a much easier time passing the review off as someone who didn't understand or simply had a different opinion on the story. In other words, we don't take it to heart about our own writing skill. More than anything, making decisions on purpose as a writer helps to protect our own mental health.

Do note, though, that even when we make decisions on purpose, we can still get readers who aren't happy. They may crave to have a dynamic character, even if you choose to make a static one.

And one more note: Static doesn't mean cardboard cutout. No one likes a character with no personality! Take James Bond as an example of a flat character. He doesn't change much from movie to movie, especially in the older ones, but he does have personality. He is observant, can read people well, is arrogant enough to do his spy job, but without being a cold-hearted bastard that no one cares about.

Children's books aside, fiction characters need to have layers to them for the story to make sense (children's books typically have one-layer characters dealing with one problem). In real life, humans are complicated creatures with ideas and beliefs that seem contradictory. And while a story isn't long enough to encompass everything a character thinks or believes, the more fittingly complicated they are, the less flat they will be.

It's this already referenced dynamic change in the character that is a large part of why there is a captivating story. But when choosing who your character will be, you must also think about how the change they will go through must be unique and true to their personality. In other words, their story development needs to honor who they are. Even the villains. If a villain suddenly makes a 180° turn, the story feels too cliché. The change that happens must mean something to them. It must make sense to their **personality**. Which you already know. Now you can compare how well your character's personality will fit within the genre.

Finding Your Character's Inner Desire

Knowing your character's inner desire (their pain point or secret or fear) is part of the arc of your character. It's talked a lot about in craft books and writing workshops and generally seen as the internal conflict of a character.

Your main character has an inner desire, or a fear, or a secret. (I use these different words to help trigger the right understanding in your writer brain.) But they, just as us in real life, have an ideal of their life and what they want to achieve, what they want to hide, what they want to become (or not).

When the reader is introduced to your character, your character *already has* this desire and inner drive. The story is about how this inner fear/want/desire comes to the forefront of your character's life. Why? Because you're about to place them into your plot. At the very beginning of the book, that point between the cover and the first page, your character is alive and well and living their life. They have no idea that the plot that you created is about to force them into a journey. Something in their life is going to interrupt their current life journey towards their own goals and desires. The plot is used to entice them towards other goals, or to make decisions they didn't think they'd have to make the day before,or it might threaten to tell their secrets.

For example, take the movie *Mean Girls*. Cady, the main character, moves from Africa to America and desires to be a "normal" high schooler. She sets off for high school, excited to be a normal kid, and then WHAM! The plot happens. Cady is pulled into a revenge plot by a girl, Janis, who claims to be her friend. The 'Plastics' aka the popular girls, used to be Janis' friend. Until they weren't.

Janis convinces Cady to become one of the 'Plastics' to spy on them. The only problem is Cady soon realizes she wants to be a 'Plastics'. She likes the attention. Soon enough Cady finds herself becoming everything she never wanted to be, culminating in a cruel prank that hurts her favorite teacher.

The climax of the plot is when Cady realizes she has become more of a mean girl than the 'Plastics', which pushes her to make the ultimate decision: will she stay the mean girl or will she learn to apologize and make up for the hurt she has caused?

The plotline of *Mean Girls* forces Cady to open her eyes to what a 'normal high-schooler' looks like. She had never been challenged on making the right decision out in the bush in Africa, but now, by the end of the story, she has to reevaluate what her inner desire really is. Does she want to be popular? Or does she want real, true friends?

In my story, *Bended Loyalty,* Tristen starts the novel wanting his band to be successful because his secret inner desire to become rich, so he never needs to fear being poor. Poverty is his monster under the bed and considers it to be the cause of all his family's problems. Of course the plot is about to make his life even more difficult and force him to reevaluate if being rich is a worthy life-goal or not.

Your Character's Backstory

One reason I split *Bended Loyalty* off from the original book and gave Tristen his own story was because I was filling the other book with too much of his backstory. While it's essential for you to know the backstory of your characters, you must avoid info dumping it onto your readers.

I highly encourage you to write out the backstory of your character in the first person. Create some key scenes in their past life that impact who they are the moment the book opens. Do this in the first person, with the character not telling a memory but the character at the age that the incidents happened. Writing it in the first person helps you get into their head on a deeper level. With this exercise you can write out all their thoughts and observations, more than you would put into the actual book, which connects you better to the inner workings of the character. It's a really fun exercise and the scenes can always be used as marketing extras for fans!

Writing these scenes out will solidify them as a real character and, I promise, you won't forget those key moments that influenced your character so deeply. This rarely happens if you just note them down in an outline.

Knowing your character's backstory will stop you from writing a generic story and instead propel you to write about a specific person struggling with a specific issue.

Once you have those key scenes written up in the first person, you can start writing the book, choosing where to include those key moments in your character's life. Instead of writing out entire scenes again, you'll be able to drop hints, or goose eggs. Just enough information for the reader to understand the backstory without needing pages and pages of information.

It's always easier said than done, so let's look at the Netflix show, *Keep Breathing*. The plotline is simple: a small plane crashes in the middle of nowhere Canada leaving Liv, the protagonist, alone to find her way home.

Through a series of flashback scenes we learn that Liv grew up with a manic-depressive mother who had abandoned the family. Liv concluded it was either her or her father's fault that her mother left, which forms her world view from a young age. She decides that allowing people in, to love them and desire their love back, wasn't worth the pain. Even when she's an adult and can rationalize this isn't true, she has already internalized her desire to keep her emotions in check, to not get attached, and certainly not fall in love. If she doesn't love anyone, then she can't be hurt.

The immediate problem for Liv is she loves her father very much and this love conflicts with her inner desire to remain unattached. We also learn that a man has entered her life that Liv sometimes wishes she could love. Problem is, as humans, we find it difficult to change our worldviews and beliefs until something happens to force us to question them. For stories, this is what the plot does: forces the character to question their world view, inner desires and beliefs of the world.

For Liv, a breakdown is about to happen. The plot is about to slam into Liv's inner desire not to be hurt. Her father is dying.

She tries to ignore the signs that he is dying, but when he breathes his last breath, her old wounds open, bringing on a breakdown and a desire to seek out her estranged mother.

But this isn't a Hallmark movie. Instead of getting to her destination for a lovely reunion, Liv's plane crashes in the Canadian wilderness leaving her alone with only her memories to comfort her. This is her moment to decide if she even wants to get home. To decide if she even *wants* to live.

In the wilderness, she struggles between her desire to give up on a world that no longer has her father and the desire to possibly give her and the man back home a chance. Before the flight, she allowed herself to get involved at a surface level with a man, refusing to fall in love with him only to find out she's pregnant just before taking the flight.

Out in the wilderness, the question she's been trying to avoid her whole life comes up over and over: should she, the daughter of a manic-depressive, be a mother? Does she deserve to be if her own mother couldn't stand to stick around? Does she deserve to be loved by her lover?

The plotline is simple: Dad dies, she goes to find mom, plane crashes, she survives the wilderness. And the world building is also simple: a forest, more or less.

What makes it a compelling story is Liv's inner struggle and her **backstory**. We don't get info dumped, though to be clear, this type of story has way more backstory than a thriller would have. We only get backstory that is relevant to moving Liv forward in the present.

Liv isn't a lovable character. She is a bitchy workaholic, and semi-alcoholic, who doesn't know a good thing when his handsome face is standing right in front of her. That kind of character is powerful, but it takes skill to make the viewer or reader care about them. Hence, the backstory.

Through flashbacks, we see her mother forgetting Liv at school or dance class. We see Liv fending for herself a lot and when her mother leaves, we see the complicated relationship between Liv and her father. Liv takes a long time to let go of her mother, but her father pulls her through and they become very close.

But while she tells herself that she doesn't care about her mother, she does. And when her father dies, she can't help but look for clues about where her mother might be.

Liv's story is even more interesting because of how bitchy, and yet sympathetic, she is as a character. We hate seeing her treat the handsome man (and father of her child), who clearly is falling in love with her, poorly. On the other hand, we sympathize that her mother messed her up. This story wouldn't be half as deep, and the ending half as satisfying, if Liv was a tenacious, hard-working woman who thrived on winning and was determined not to let anything beat her down. Not her mom. Not even the forest. With Liv, we have a character who is hard-working and tenacious, but she is also struggling with whether it's worth her beating the forest. She is constantly asking herself if she should just give up.

In *Keep Breathing*, we have the personality the writers created for Liv, plus her inner desire, together with her backstory, create an engaging tale, that would otherwise be a woman walking through the woods. We come to understand Liv and even root for this bitchy lawyer every time she makes the decision to live. The ending is fulfilling because by then we know her history and we celebrate with her when she decides to accept that which cannot be changed and instead change her view of life in order to get the most out of it.

Do you see what I mean when I say that character development is so much more than knowing how your character looks, what size she is and what her favorite food is? It's everything all together, all at once!

Find Your Character's Flaw

Characters have to have at least one flaw. This will get in their way all the time. It might be a big part of the novel's theme or it might not, but it will be part of who they are as a character. It will also be why people remember them. Let's go back to *Mean Girls*. One of Cady's flaws is that she's willing to do whatever it takes to be accepted by girls her own age. And she's taken advantage of both by the "uncool" kids and by the most popular girls. She doesn't know herself and it's this willingness to do what they want her to do that gets her in trouble.

In *Legally Blonde*, Elle's flaw is believing people are like her: upstanding and big-hearted. And she gets taken for a ride all the time because of this flaw.

What is a flaw? Well, your character can be naïve to the world. Or lack patience. They can believe they are the most handsome guy around and everyone should treat them special because of it. They could be a doormat for everyone. Be jaded. They can be prejudiced, or a man/woman hater. Perhaps they believe they're always right. Or they're too proud, or a slob or OCD. Perhaps they are unmotivated or overly motivated. Too optimistic or too pessimistic. They don't love themselves or they love themselves too much.

The reason it's important to know your character's flaw is that they react to the world, the other characters and the plot happening around them, from the flaw vantage point. If they are prejudiced and placed with someone from another demographic, they need to be reacting to this situation according to their prejudice.

If your character loves themselves more than they love others, you need to show that in their speech and how they react to those around them as the plot moves them forward.

The plot will force your character to confront their flaw so knowing what the flaw is and understanding how someone with that flaw would act, think, and behave will make your story richer.

Now that you've done the hard work of deciding on personalities, written a sketch of their backstory, figured out what your character's inner desire and flaw is, it's time to put it all into practice.

Above all: Honor the character as you, the writer, set them up from the beginning.

Our characters need to grow and mature, but they need to be essentially the same person at the end of the story. Why? Because all the rest of us real humans are essentially the same person even after we have learned something new. We are still recognizable to the world even after becoming sober, or finding love, or no longer being prejudiced, or (place all the flaws and inner lies we have here).

We want to see that the main character is recognizable, too. So don't veer off the path and make a completely different person for the end of the story. It was enough work just to make the interesting, complicated character for the beginning! Stay with that character, stick them in the plotline arc and you'll be on your way.

Top Ten Countdown to finding the core of your character

So here are my top ten exercises to develop the sketch of your character that's in your head and get it onto paper.

10. Go people watching in order to create a new character.

We want to see the personality of our characters in action. People watching is great for character inspiration or for finding that important tick, emotional response or thought process your character needs to come alive on the page.

Observing real people in life can help us write believable hand gestures or facial expressions to show the reader what the character is feeling or going through or thinking.

9. Reacting in stressful situations.

Place your character into extraordinarily stressful situations such as a car accident or a loved one leaving/dying. Or perhaps getting yelled at in the store. You know their personality now and have observed people like them in real life, so now it's time to write them in a reactionary scene. **This might or might not make it into your book.** This is an exercise to get deeper with your character. Once you've written the scene, turn it around and write it from a different angle to stretch your character further.

Be conscious of how your character would react and stay true to their personality, even if it grates you the wrong way. One of the biggest traps is to make your character always have the perfect thing to say. That just isn't real life.

. . .

8. Create a group conversation around dinner.

It can be about anything really, but make it a situation in which a group has to make a decision. Write what emotional state your main character is entering the scene in. Write what they hope to achieve from this scene (a full belly? Or a seat next to the cute, new guys, etc.) Then write it in the first person from your character's point of view, writing out their thoughts. Then write it in the third person and try to put these thoughts on the page without using inner, italicized dialogue. Use instead their hand movements, their facial expressions and their interpretation of those around them. How does your character behave? Be conscious of how you've developed this character and make sure their reactions make sense.

7. Find out their backstory by writing it in first person.

Place them in the past *inside* the situation that caused their formation. Knowing what happened to your character to form them into the character that appears on the page is great, but writing out the entire scene from the first person perspective is even better. It doesn't have to be perfectly written, but getting into their younger head helps cement their view of the world in your writer's head. You can then reference this scene in richer context throughout the story.

6. Write your character's everyday schedule and how they would react if it were interrupted.

Write a scene with them explaining their routine and someone pushing back on it. Your character has to defend their routine. Or perhaps they're a pushover and they allow the other person to convince them to change, even though they like their routine. Dig into the inner thoughts of your character. Don't worry about being cheesy, this is about really getting to know your character.

5. Write the ending.

Go directly to how you see your novel ending if they get their inner desire. Everything they claim they've always wanted. How do they react? Is it good enough? Why or why not?

Now write a scene where they DON'T get what they thought they wanted most. How does it affect them? Would they see the world differently? Would their life be terrible?

In both scenarios, the character should learn something.

4. Create a sidekick or best friend.

Write out a scene where the main character meets this sidekick for the first time. Or write a scene in which they have an encounter with someone else together. The sidekick or best friend should bring out the best in your main character without sounding preachy.

3. Write a letter from your character to a friend or lover.

Write this letter in the first person and have your character reflect on themselves and the surrounding situation. You could also experiment with writing letters from your character as an older person, years after the plot of your story has already affected them. What would they say?

2. Write your character's obituary.

A bit morbid, but fun to do. What is your character known for? Are they beloved? Do they leave any loved ones behind? How many people show up to the funeral?

1. Write diary entries of several life events.

First kiss. First love. First job. First house. Whatever life events you can think of, try to write a diary entry for them. Get into their voice. Only write what they would write.

Meet Kat Caldwell

Kat Caldwell believes that each person on earth has a story to tell. Kat is a storyteller in her own right, having written a historical novel, *Stepping Across the Desert* and a magical realm novel, *An Audience with the King*, as well as a creative coach and podcaster. In between coaching clients, interviewing creatives for the Pencils&Lipstick podcast and writing her next novel, you can find Kat traveling the world, studying another language, reading a good book or volunteering at her local church—with a cup of cold brew close by.

You can find out more about Kat and her work at:

https://katcaldwell.com/

https://www.facebook.com/katcaldwellauthor

https://www.instagram.com/katcaldwell.author/

Show & Tell: The Key to Engaging and Meaningful Storytelling

Heather Davis

There's an insidious piece of writing advice that has been making the rounds for decades (maybe longer) and, if you've been reading craft books for any length of time, I'm sure you've heard it once or twice: Show Don't Tell.

If you're not familiar with the saying, Show Don't Tell is a writing technique that encourages writers to immerse readers in a scene using sensory details and actions instead of using exposition to blandly summarize the events. This is supposed to keep readers engaged and prevent the dreaded "info dumping" that would be a more effective sleep aid than melatonin.

At first blush, this advice sounds pretty good. In fact, Show Don't Tell has become the unofficial mantra of practically every writer looking to create powerful, impactful prose.

After all, why *wouldn't* it be a good idea to write like a video camera and Show readers what's going on? How else are they ever going to create a clear image of the scene in their heads?

But the truth about engaging storytelling is, unfortunately, far more complex than this mantra leads writers to believe. If taken too literally, Show Don't Tell will keep your novel in a literary agent's slush pile forever. Even worse? Readers will never connect with your protagonist or finish your novel. Yikes.

> *But wait*, you say. *If Show Don't Tell is such terrible advice, why are so many authors and editors touting it?*

This is complicated, but I think there are two main reasons. First, many writers and editors misunderstand what makes the human brain crave stories. Second, when truly talented authors and editors pass along this questionable advice, they are most likely being misunderstood.

Why? Because readers must deeply connect with the protagonist in order to care about the story—and that cannot be accomplished through showing alone.

How the Brain Constructs Meaning: The Emotions Behind Engaging Stories

What does it mean to weave an engaging tale? You're probably picturing action-packed car chases, flamboyant sword fights, and oh-so-delectable banter between potential romantic partners. While these exciting events may seem like just the thing your novel needs, there's a certain amount of danger in assuming that action equals engagement.

According to neuroeconomist Paul Zak, who did a series of experiments aimed at understanding what makes people respond to stories, there are two emotions that readers must feel to remain focused on a story: distress and empathy.

To understand how these emotions relate to the creation of engaging novels, let's quickly review story structure.

Way back in the 19th century, novelist Gustav Freytag developed the now-famous narrative pyramid. The narrative pyramid was divided into five key stages: exposition, rising action, climax, falling action, and resolution. These story stages combine to create what's called a Dramatic Arc. And no matter which story structure guide you seek to implement in your writing (the Three Act Structure, the Hero's Journey, etc.) you will still find the Dramatic Arc at its core.

Now let's return to Zak's experiments. Zak's team showed viewers one of two short films. The first film included images of a father and his young son at the zoo. The father narrated the events, but the story was a simple vignette with no Dramatic Arc. The second film, however, included images of the father and son interacting in a hospital setting. This time, the narration conveyed more context and emotional revelation. The father confided that his son was dying of cancer and, though the little boy felt good enough to play, the father struggled to interact with his son because he knew the child would soon die. By the end of the video, however, the father resolved to find joy in the finite time he had left with his son.

Zak's experiment included physical evidence of human response to the story. His team drew participant's blood before and after they viewed the films and assayed the samples for the presence of several specific hormones, including oxytocin and cortisol. Oxytocin is associated with complex emotions such as love, trust, and empathy. Cortisol is associated with emotional distress and focused attention. Study participants who viewed the first film did not show an increase in levels of oxytocin or cortisol, but those who viewed the second film showed a substantial increase in both hormones. Meaning, the first film did not cause viewers to feel much of anything, but the second film entangled them in emotion. Viewers felt both distress and empathy. And, because of those emotions, they were significantly more likely to donate their hard-earned money to cancer research after viewing the film.

This is a fascinating finding because it points to why certain novels resonate and others do not. Essentially, it tells us what feelings motivate people to focus on a story and take action as a result.

But why did the second film have an impact when the first did not? What was the most important difference between the two stories? It certainly wasn't a fancy action sequence because neither film relied on visually dramatic events. The answer, then, is simple: the second film had backstory and meaning. The father's deeply personal narration gave viewers context about the son's illness and explored the father's emotional struggle. Viewers, armed with that pivotal information, began to feel connected to the father and son, and they wanted to see the father overcome his struggle and find a measure of peace.

But what does this mean for writers? Good question! It means that dazzling readers with an exciting plot will only take you half the distance. If you truly want to change the hearts and minds of readers (and hopefully motivate them to buy books), you must Show what's happening in the External World of the novel, and then you must connect those events back to the Internal World of the protagonist. By doing this, you employ the subtle art of "Show and Tell" storytelling to bamboozle readers into feeling both distress and empathy for your characters. And readers, marinating in a delicious cocktail of hormones, are hooked from the very first sentence.

Showing to Convey Meaning: The Subtle Art of Establishing the Protagonist's External World

You are a writer, and you are writing a novel. However, for a moment, let's pretend you are making a movie instead, shall we? Let's pretend that it's your job to film each scene in your book, but instead of just being the camera person, you're also the director, so it's your job to tell the actors *exactly* what to do and when to do it. Every nod of the head, wave, grimace, and crooked smile must be orchestrated by *you*. But that's not all! You're also the costume designer, the lighting person, and set builder. Oh yeah, and you wrote the script, too.

This, in essence, is Showing—putting words on the page that will paint a picture of the protagonist's External World in the minds of readers. Showing is a combination of physical descriptions (of people, locations, and actions), character body language, and dialog. Showing is about engaging the senses—sights, sounds, smells, tastes, and sensations—to draw readers' attention to important information that will help them understand the meaning of the story. But here's the thing —Showing is about a lot more than just "becoming a video camera." It's about choosing the right words to describe the right details so you can create *meaning* in the minds of your readers.

You can't (and shouldn't) try to describe *everything*, of course. That would be a chaotic mess of useless information. Instead, you must carefully select the details you deem worthy of description so that each word you put on the page adds value to the scene and the novel as a whole.

Showing Through Sensory Information

Descriptions involving the five senses can provide readers with valuable information about the meaning of a scene and help them feel like they are a part of the action.

In the novel *The Invisible Life of Addie Larue*, author V.E. Schwab uses sensory information extensively as a tool to establish mood and narrow the focus of the scene. Let's explore the sensory information given in the passage below.

> *When it is over, she collapses, breathless, into the sheets beside him,*
> *sweat and rain chilling on her skin. Henry folds around her, pulls*

her back into the circle of his warmth, and she can feel his heart slowing through his ribs, a metronome easing back into its measure.

The room goes quiet, marked only by the steady rain beyond the windows, a drowsy aftermath of passion, and soon she can feel him drifting down toward sleep.

Addie looks up at the ceiling.

"Don't forget," she says softly, the words half prayer, half plea.

Can you intuit the urgency and intensity of the moment? Can you feel the chill of the rain and the warmth of the embrace? Can you hear the rain? Of course, you can! You were, in fact, transported *into* the moment. You became part of the unfolding scene.

That is the power of slowing the moment down and drawing from the senses.

Showing Through Use of Description

Descriptions of the External World are important to your novel for several reasons. First, and most obviously, they help you build the world your protagonist lives in. And, even if you're not writing science fiction or fantasy, you don't get a free pass on world building. No matter which genre or category of fiction you write, you *still* need to use your words to construct a world that feels authentic. For example, I am working with a client whose novel is about a rock band rising to fame in the 1960s. Although some of his readers may be old enough to remember this era, most are not. So, my client must create this world every bit as meticulously as a fantasy author would create an alien world across the galaxy.

But descriptions are about far more than just matter-of-factly telling readers what something looks like or sounds like, etc. Descriptions are actually a secret (and powerful) tool in your arsenal that can be used to help your reader decode the meaning of your scenes.

Let's imagine something simple like a man pulling into his driveway and looking at his house. A writer could simply picture the scene in their mind and succinctly describe it as follows:

> *Nick pulled into the driveway and looked at the house, which sat in darkness.*

Technically, there's nothing wrong with that passage... but it lacks oomph, and it doesn't set the mood or convey the underlying emotional meaning of the scene to come. It's only doing *half* its job!

Now let's take a look at how Amanda Prowse wrote this passage in her brilliant novel *The Light in the Hallway.*

> *Nick pulled up onto the steep driveway and looked at the house, which sat shaded forlornly in the soft bruise of darkness.*

Notice the difference? This second passage conveys mood and emotion through word choice. Prowse carefully selected descriptors like *steep, forlornly,* and *soft bruise of darkness* to highlight the sad, heavy feeling of the scene about to begin. She's not just describing the house for the sake of describing the house. Instead, she's using the description of the house as a tool to convey deeper meaning.

Now let's examine an example where author Kristin Hannah uses weather to convey mood and meaning in her novel *The Great Alone.*

> *In January, the weather got worse. Cold and darkness isolated the Allbright family even more. Feeding the woodstove became priority number one, a constant round-the-clock chore.... And as if all of that weren't stressful enough, on bad nights—nightmare nights—Dad*

woke them in the middle of the night to pack and repack their bug-out bags, to test their preparedness, to take their weapons apart and put them back together.

Notice how Hannah is using the weather to emphasize how the Allbright family is entering a dark and isolated time? Imagine if she wrote the following sentence instead: *In January, the weather got better. Warmth and sunlight seemed to crack open the days.* That alternative starting point probably feels jarring, right? That's because it doesn't provide the subtle clues that readers need to decode the scene.

Describing characters can also be a powerful way to provide readers with meaning. First, let's get this out of the way: you don't need every physical detail about your characters. Instead, cherry pick specific aspects of a character's physical appearance to give readers a better window into the character's personality or role in the story. And choose words that will highlight your meaning.

Let's look at a passage from *The House on the Cerulean Sea* by T.J. Klune to see this in action.

Ms. Jenkins reached his desk, her mouth a thin line. As was her wont, she appeared to have applied her makeup rather liberally in the dark without the benefit of a mirror. The heavy rouge on her cheeks was magenta, and her lipstick looked like blood. She wore a black pantsuit, the buttons of which were closed all the way up to just under her chin. She was thin as a dream, made up of sharp bones covered in skin stretched too tightly.

Notice how Klune cleverly tells readers exactly how they are supposed to feel about (and what to expect from) Ms. Jenkins before she utters her first word? The description of Ms. Jenkins is filled with harsh, brash words and sharp similes and metaphors. Ms. Jenkin's physical description becomes a window into her character, and thus is not really about her exterior at all—it's about giving readers a window into her interior so they know how to feel about her actions and the effect she will exert on the story.

Showing Through Characters' Body Language

Body language is powerful because it can give readers an instant window into basic emotions. Even better, it's nearly impossible to consciously control body language (at least in a convincing way), which means you use body language in two ways. First, body language can be used to accentuate characters' emotions. Second, you can use body language to Show a discrepancy between what a character wants others to *think* they're feeling and what they are *actually* feeling. Because of this, body language can be used to layer in subtext and thus give rise to tension and suspense.

Let's take a look at how Celeste Ng plays with body language to convey meaning in her novel *Everything I Never Told You*.

> *"I'm sorry."*
>
> *"Sorry? For what? There's nothing to be sorry about."* Lydia slung the bag over her shoulder. *"Actually, I'm sorry for you. In love with someone who hates you."*
>
> *She glared at Jack: one sharp wince, as if she'd splashed water in his eyes. Then Jack's face grew wary and pinched and closed, like it was with other people, like it had been the first day they'd met. He grinned, but it looked more like a grimace.*
>
> *"At least I don't let other people tell me what I want," he said, and she flinched at the contempt in his voice.*

In this scene, Ng provides dialog that is slightly out-of-tune with body language, building tension and indicating to readers that Lydia is not unphased by Jack's transgression. Even though she says, "I'm actually sorry for you," it is obvious that she means to hurt him with her words. Jack's facial expressions confirm that that happened and, when he grinned afterward, it is grimace-like, indicating that Jack is not actually happy; he's ready to verbally strike back. This is a perfect example of using body language to add texture and depth to a scene.

Showing Through Dialog

Dialog is absolutely pivotal to stories. First, it speeds up the perceived pace of the scene, which allows readers to feel the momentum of the narrative. Second, it is a tool writers use to fully immerse readers in a scene, by zooming in the focus. It can be powerful in terms of creating moments of subtext that lead to larger perceptions of tension and suspense. Third, you can use dialog to Tell readers a *lot* about your characters through the way they express themselves.

Let's look at an example of well-crafted dialog written by Phoebe Fox in *The Way We Weren't.*

> *"What kind of trouble are you in?"*
>
> *"What? I'm not—"*
>
> *"Bullshit. Don't mess with me, girl. I've been dealing with liars longer than you've been alive. You can tell me the truth, or I can call the cops and let you explain it to them. Your choice."*

What can we discern from the above exchange? Well, we know that the "girl" is hiding something that she doesn't want to talk about— something the police would be interested in, no less. We know that she's interacting with a crotchety, no-nonsense person who is much older than she. Also, from the tone of the older person's language, we might guess that this person is a man. We *also* might guess that the crotchety old man is not the reserved, scholarly type. He seems like more of a working-class Joe. Wow. That's a lot of information readers can pick up from three little lines of dialog!

When writing dialog, remember that you are accessing a powerful tool, but there are some important rules that must be observed in order to keep your dialog on track and reader friendly.

The Six Golden Rules of Dialog

1. Avoid talking heads. Instead, use dialog tags and/or relevant character actions to tie spoken lines seamlessly back to the speaker.
2. Start a new paragraph when the speaker changes. This creates clarity and increases momentum.
3. Keep dialog relatively short. Remember: a conversation is an *exchange*, not a monologue or a lecture.
4. Let the dialog sound natural. People don't typically speak in full sentences. Also, make sure the word choice reflects the age of the speaker. Children do not speak like teens, who do not speak like twenty-somethings, who do not speak like adults, etc.
5. Create subtext by letting the characters avoid saying things directly. Let's be 100% honest. People don't typically say exactly what they're thinking. For example, your partner might say they are fine when they are *definitely* not fine. So, make sure that your characters don't always just come right out and say what's on their minds—especially in emotionally fraught situations.
6. Ensure that dialog gives readers a deeper understanding of the characters and the situation. Dialog can immediately convey information about age, social class, educational level,

emotion, plot-level events, and so much more. Make sure you're using dialog to do all of this important work.

Telling to Convey Meaning: The Subtle Art of Revealing the Protagonist's Internal World

Telling has a seriously *bad* reputation in the literary world. Why? Because when used incorrectly, it can be a snoozefest that stands in the way of readers connecting with the story. However, if used in the *right* way, it is the key to readers understanding the meaning of the story.

From a story perspective, Showing and Telling are perfect partners. First, we Show readers what happens in the external, "video camera" version of the novel, and then, using the idiosyncratic filter of the protagonist's thoughts, we Tell them why what happened actually mattered. In essence, the protagonist's perspective becomes the decoder ring necessary for readers to understand the importance of the plot level events.

Because Telling is about interpretation and meaning, it is non-negotiable if you want readers to connect with your novel.

Telling Through Backstory (Context, Memory, and Flashback)

Many writers and editors warn against backstory because they want to help new writers avoid the dreaded info dump. Unfortunately, the idea of stripping a novel of backstory will do nothing but create a work that is as bland and lifeless as plain rice cakes. Also, it completely strips the story of texture, depth, and meaning. Why? Because as William Faulkner famously wrote, "The past is never dead. It's not even past." And this psychological foible is as true for your protagonist as it is for real people.

Why? Because everything that happens in the Story Present is tied to the protagonist's understanding and motivations that arose from the Story Past. For example: why is the protagonist trying to get a million Twitter followers? Because he thinks that fame means success. Why does he think that fame means success? Because his father was once a famous actor who began drinking heavily when his movie roles dwindled, and the acting world forgot about him. Why did his father's drinking have an impact on him? Because it tore apart the family. See how fast we got from what the protagonist wants in the Story Present to the scars inflicted on them in the Story Past?

There are three forms of backstory: context, memory, and flashback. Before we jump into examples of each, let's establish a few simple rules that hold true for *all* forms of backstory.

Three Golden Rules of Backstory

1. Backstory should be clear, specific, and concrete. When giving backstory, specificity is key, and "general" is the kiss of death... and thus should be avoided at all costs.
2. Backstory should be tied to something in the Story Present. Meaning, there should be a clear reason why the Story Present is causing the protagonist to think back about the Story Past.
3. Backstory should illuminate something about the Story Present. If you are going to divulge backstory, there should be a *reason*! There should be something specific about the Story Present that would remain confusing (or at least unclear) without the insight that is provided by knowing the Story Past.

Weaving in Context to Convey Meaning

Context is what your protagonist knows about the world. The truth as they see it. How things are. Their place in the world and how the world functions. Context, therefore, is key to readers' understanding of what's going on in the scene, and, because of this, should be used liberally.

Here's an example of context in *The Hate You Give* by Angie Thomas.

> *"Starr Amara," she says through her teeth. Since my first name is only one syllable, she has to throw my middle name in there to break it down. "If you don't hand me that phone, I swear to God."*

I open my mouth, but she goes, "Say something else! I dare you, say something else! I'll take them Jordans too!"

This is some bullshit. For real. Daddy watches us; her attack dog, waiting for us to make a wrong move. That's how they work. Momma does the first round, and if it's not successful, Daddy does for the KO. And you never want Daddy to go for the KO.

Seven and I hand her our phones.

Thomas doesn't just Show the argument between Starr and her parents. Instead, she goes deeper and does an incredible job of giving readers context around what these arguments are typically like. We also get a sense of how unfair Starr finds this arrangement. Context like this not only enriches the narrative, but also provides readers the necessary information they need to understand why Starr makes the decision to hand over her phone without further protest. Without this context, readers would be left with only a general idea of what motivates Starr.

Weaving in Memory or Flashback to Convey Meaning

Memories and Flashbacks are ways writers can directly give readers a window into the Story Past. When I use the term "memory," I am referencing shorter snippets of the Story Past. During memories, the protagonist stays firmly anchored in the Story Present. When I use the term "flashbacks," I am referencing longer chunks of Story Past. Flashbacks are typically full scenes plucked from the Story Past and delivered as an intact unit.

However, since these two elements are quite similar except in length and anchor, we will consider them together.

Memories and flashbacks go further than context. They are specific, concrete, and clear. They pull from one very precise time in the past and explore it in greater depth so that it can help illuminate something about the present. Often, memories and flashbacks include dialog, sensory information, and many other Show and Tell techniques because they are, in fact, fragments of scenes.

Let's examine a passage from *Tell the Wolves I'm Home* by Carol Rifka Brunt. In this passage, memory is seamlessly inserted to give readers important insight into the close relationship between June—the protagonist—and her uncle Finn, who is dying of AIDS.

> *That afternoon we sat for an hour and a half while Finn painted us. He had on Mozart's Requiem, which Finn and I both loved....*
>
> *The Requiem was a secret between me and Finn. Just the two of us. We didn't even need to look at each other when he put it on. We both understood. He'd taken me to a concert at a beautiful church on 84th Street once and told me to close my eyes and listen. That's when I first heard it. That's when I first fell in love with that music.*
>
> *"It creeps up on you, doesn't it?" he'd said. "It lulls you into thinking it's pleasant and harmless, it bumbles along, then all of a sudden, boom, there it is rising up all menacing. All big drums and high screaming strings and deep dark voices. Then just as fast it backs right down again. See, Crocodile? See?"*

In the above passage, readers start in the present moment: Uncle Finn is painting June and her sister. But when Uncle Finn puts on *Requiem*, the author provides context, which quickly lapses into memory. The memory then illuminates the Story Present, providing readers a better understanding of the deep bond between June and her uncle. When used in this way, backstory helps a writer create a rich and deeply textured world that resonates with readers.

Telling Through the Protagonist's Thoughts, Feelings, Fears, and Internal Debate

Very often the protagonist just needs to T*ell* readers what the heck is going on inside their head. This ability to lay bare the Internal World of the protagonist—their thoughts, feelings, fears and internal debates, etc.— is actually the singular beauty of novels. Unlike TV and movies, readers sink into the mind of the protagonist. They see the world as the protagonist sees it, which is not like a video camera at all. No way! It's actually more like a funhouse mirror, all skewed and distorted and unique to the protagonist.

And that's why we readers *love* novels, isn't it? Novels transport us to the private world of another human being. We are finally able to know what another person thinks and feels. We are so close, in fact, that we actually *merge* with the protagonist, *becoming* them for a short period of time.

Let's see this magic in action in a scene from Suzanne Collins' novel *The Ballad of Songbirds and Snakes.*

> *"Let's all kill him," the tiny boy said viciously. "Can't do nothing worse to us."*
>
> *Several other tributes murmured in agreement and took a step in.*
>
> *Coriolanus went rigid with fear. Kill him? Did they really mean to beat him to death, right here in broad daylight, in the middle of the Capitol? Suddenly, he knew they did. What, after all, did they have to lose? His heart pounded in his chest, and he crouched slightly, fists extended, in anticipation of the imminent attack.*

Notice all the things going on in the scene above. There's definitely some Showing in the form of dialog (the tiny boy suggests killing

Coriolanus) and action (the tributes murmur and step forward, indicating they are ready to attack). But after that Showing, Collins immediately lets her protagonist do some necessary Telling. She doesn't start out with "his heart pounded in his chest." Instead, she starts by saying that he went rigid with fear. His emotion is directly named. She then lets Coriolanus make sense of what's happening to him *on the page* for readers to experience. The focus of this scene is tightly zoomed in, and readers feel like they are standing inside of Coriolanus' shoes, facing off against the tributes.

Imagine if Collins had stripped away Coriolanus' internal ruminations. The scene would have read like this:

> *"Let's all kill him," the tiny boy said viciously. "Can't do nothing worse to us."*
>
> *Several other tributes murmured in agreement and took a step in.*
>
> *Coriolanus' heart pounded in his chest, and he crouched slightly, fists extended, in anticipation of the imminent attack.*

Notice how *thin* and *flat* that feels? By stripping away the Internal World of the protagonist, I have robbed the scene of its power. I have essentially locked readers out of the real story—which is how the plot affects the protagonist.

Getting it on the Page

Now that you understand the importance of Showing and Telling in your prose, it's important to get it *on the page* as you write. Unfortunately, this is often the place where writers stumble.

Why? Because writers have the "curse of knowledge" when it comes to their own stories. The narrative is so vivid and clear in their own heads, that they imagine they've actually put all that important information on the page. Their brains, in fact, automatically "fill in the blanks." But when this happens in a burgeoning novel, it is very disconcerting to readers. To them, the narrative feels like a puzzle with key pieces missing, and they can't quite extrapolate the lost information, which makes them frustrated and ready to slam the book closed forever.

To help solve this problem, I have one piece of advice for writers: constantly ask yourself *why*. *Why* is the character saying this line of dialog? *Why* is this event happening? *Why* is this character feeling what they're feeling? *Why* is this character doing what they're doing? *Why* is this event impacting the protagonist? *Why* is this happening now?

After you've asked yourself *why* until the word sounds wrong in your ears, weave the answers to all those *whys* into your story to help readers decode the narrative. If you do this consistently, your novel will develop a strong cause-and-effect trajectory and powerful emotional continuity.

By Showing *and* Telling, you will mesmerize readers by creating the unique amalgam of emotions that lure them into the satisfying arms of a well-told story.

Top Ten Countdown

Below are ten key questions to ask yourself whenever you write a scene. These questions will ensure that you are both *Showing* readers what's happening in the external world, but also *Telling* them why it matters to your protagonist. In short, these questions guarantee that you impart meaning to your prose so readers and agents are hooked from the very first sentence.

10. Are you carefully describing the External World (locations, characters, objects, weather, etc.) using words that indicate mood, tone, and meaning?

9. Are you sprinkling in sensory information (sight, sound, smell, taste, touch) so that readers feel fully immersed in the unfolding events?

8. Are you using dialog naturally and ensuring it is freckled with subtext to help generate suspense and tension?

7. Are you using body language to layer in subtext and build suspense and tension?

6. Does your protagonist have a unique, idiosyncratic perspective that shines through on every page?

5. Is your protagonist mentally referencing their backstory to help them understand the Story Present and to make decisions?

4. Is it clear what your protagonist thinks and feels about what is happening in each scene?

3. Is it clear what your protagonist *fears* will happen next?

2. Are your characters acting and reacting logically to the events in the plot so that they seem like real people with authentic emotions and motivations?

1. Are you constantly asking yourself *why* your protagonist is thinking, feeling, behaving, and communicating the way you have portrayed them in the scene? And, more importantly, have you put the answers to those "whys" on the page so that the reader fully understands your protagonist's motivations?

Meet Heather Davis

Dr. Heather Davis is a storyteller, Author Accelerator certified book coach, certified copy editor, author platform expert, and the founder of *The Kreative Authorpreneur*. She helps aspiring diversity authors create emotionally complex novels that readers rave about and agents request.

Heather has studied under story experts Lisa Cron and Jennie Nash. She is a frequent contributor to Jane Friedman's popular writing blog and has been featured on podcasts such as Editing Writing and Turning Readers into Writers. In October of 2022, Heather hosted a writing workshop inside Alexa Bigwarfe's wildly popular Women In Publishing (WIP) School.

Heather lives on the Eastern Shore of Maryland where she loves trail running, sipping iced mocha lattes, and bingeing Audiobooks like some people binge Netflix. She is currently entangled in the process of editing her first novel (with the expert help of her own phenomenal book coach, of course).

Find out more about Heather and her work at:

https://thekreativeauthorpreneur.com/

https://twitter.com/HLeeDavisWriter

https://www.linkedin.com/in/heather-davis-phd-7221b215a/

Start Cleaning Up Your Novel With These Grammar and Punctuation Tips

Stacy Juba

Creating compelling characters, vivid scenes, and startling plot twists are the fun parts of writing a novel. Most authors love tapping into their imagination and coaxing a story to life on the page.

Writing and editing has a technical side, however, that some consider drudge work. Fixing all the grammar and punctuation mistakes can be tedious and difficult, depending on the author's skill level. No matter how well-written your book is, having it riddled with errors will leave a bad impression on readers. Manuscripts with poor copy-editing and proofreading are branded as amateur and unprofessional.

If you struggle with grammar and punctuation, the good news is that with self-study and a few helpful tools, you can improve. Let's dive into eight of the biggest problem areas for writers.

Noun Capitalization

Back in elementary school, we learned that a noun was a person, place, or thing. You might have forgotten, though, that we can break down this category even further.

Common nouns are the generic name for a person, place, or thing in a class or group. For example: *aunt, uncle, beach, building, movie.* Common nouns are not capitalized unless they begin a sentence.

Proper nouns name an individual person, place, company, or organization and require capitalization. They can also refer to the titles of books, films, songs, and other media. Note the differences: *Aunt Betty, Uncle John, Venice Beach, the Empire State Building,* and *The Hunger Games.* Here we're referring to a specific aunt, uncle, beach, building, and movie.

This general vs. specific concept also extends to titles for a person, which can confuse authors who need to brush up on capitalization. Some beginner manuscripts will have references to the *Admiral, the Vice President, the Judge,* or *the Chief.* Since these titles are generic and don't refer to a particular admiral, vice president, judge, or chief, these are common nouns and should be lowercase.

That changes if you're talking about a specific person. *Admiral Halsey, Vice President Harris, Judge Wapner,* or *Chief Wallace* are proper nouns and need capitalization. The same goes for directly addressing someone, e.g. "Good morning, **Captain**. Hello, **Judge**."

Don't underestimate the importance of capitalization. Learn the differences between common and proper nouns.

The Oxford Comma

Another question posed by many writers is: what the heck is the Oxford Comma and when should it be used? Also called a serial comma, the Oxford Comma is the final comma in a list of three or more items.

For example:

- I had a ham sandwich, chips**, and** an apple for lunch.

- Do you want pasta salad, coleslaw**,** **or** a garden salad?

Unfortunately, some writers are inconsistent with their use of the Oxford Comma. One sentence will include it and another will leave it out, e.g. They went to the mall, the park **and** out to dinner.

Notice how in the above example, there is no comma between *park* and *out to dinner*.

So, which method is correct?

That depends. Most publishers follow a style guide, which means they have set rules for how authors should use language and punctuation. This ensures consistency across every book in the publisher's catalog and every article in a particular newspaper or magazine.

Popular style guides include *The Chicago Manual of Style*, the *MLA Handbook*, and the *AP Stylebook*. If you're contracted with a publisher, check to see whether they use the Oxford Comma.

If you plan to self-publish or submit to agents and publishers, then the decision is yours. Pick one style and stick with it throughout the entire manuscript.

Other Comma Uses

Commas are the Achilles heel of writers around the globe. The Oxford Comma is just one concept to understand. There are many other rules regarding commas, and this little punctuation mark often causes big mistakes.

In a nutshell, commas represent a short pause and are used to divide parts of a sentence. Here are a few rules to keep in mind.

Use a comma after an introductory word, phrase, or clause to give the reader a slight breather. For example:

- Whenever we go out **trick-or-treating**, I give the kids a pillowcase and a flashlight.
- **Fortunately,** the forecast looks nice for the party.
- After I put away the **groceries,** I made dinner.
- **However**, I don't know what time I'll be home.
- **Yes**, I'd love to go with you.

Use a comma before ***for, and, nor, but, or, yet,*** *or* ***so*** *to join two independent clauses that form a compound sentence.* You can use the acronym *FANBOYS* to remember the words. Here are some examples:

- I left the party early, **for** I was very tired.
- I'll read your book**, and** I'm sure I will enjoy it.
- Nancy didn't return my call**, nor** did she respond to my email.
- I knocked on her door, **but** no one answered.
- She will either order spaghetti and meatballs, **or** a burger and fries.

Use a pair of commas in the middle of a sentence to set off clauses, phrases, and words that are not essential to the meaning of the sentence. For example:

Next Monday, **my day off from work,** is the only day I can meet for lunch.

My daughter, **wearing her princess costume,** is playing in the corner.

Jake**, the best player on the hockey team,** scored the game-winning goal.

Vanilla ice cream**, which is my favorite flavor,** is what I use to make milkshakes.

My grandfather, **who had a heart attack last year,** watches his cholesterol and exercises.

Colons

Colons and semicolons are two more punctuation marks that can baffle writers. Some authors assume they are interchangeable, or incorrectly opt for a comma. A *colon* is used to introduce a description, an explanation, or a list. Usually, when you see a colon in a sentence, it implies *as follows*, *which is/are*, or *thus*. Here are some examples:

Introducing a list.

- I always pack these medical items when I go on vacation**: a thermometer**, vitamins, and inhaler.

Note: Only capitalize the first item in the list if it's a proper noun. For example:

- When you go to New York City, make sure to visit these attractions**: Radio City Music Hall**, the Statue of Liberty, and the Empire State Building.

Between independent clauses when the second illustrates or explains the first. It is your choice whether to use the colon in these instances. A period would work also.

- Jill deserved the college **scholarship: she** maintained an A average for four years.

Or

- Jill deserved the college **scholarship. She** maintained an A average for four years.

For emphasis. Again, it is your choice whether to use a colon or period.

- Lindsay jumped up from her seat as the puck flew into the net**: score!**

Or

- Lindsay jumped up from her seat as the puck flew into the net. **Score!**

Semicolons

A *semicolon* is used between two parts of a sentence, usually when each part could form a grammatical sentence on its own. It shows a pause more pronounced than that indicated by a comma. A semi-colon can also separate the items in a list.

Here are some semicolon guidelines:

· · ·

Links two independent clauses closely related in thought, giving them equal weight. These are two sentences melded together, which is why you can't use a comma. Since they could be complete sentences, you have the option of using a period.

- Thomas went to baseball **practice; his** brother went to track practice.

Or

- Thomas went to baseball **practice. His** brother went to track practice.

Helps a conjunctive adverb join two independent clauses. Conjunctive adverbs include *nevertheless, however, therefore, otherwise, also, then, finally, likewise, indeed,* and *consequently.* Since these clauses could be complete sentences, a period would work here also.

- I tried to call in sick to work**; however**, it wasn't my fault that the line was busy for a half hour.

Or

- I tried to call in sick to work**. However**, it wasn't my fault that the line was busy for a half hour.

Used in a long serial list with several commas.

- Danny bought pajamas, slippers, and fuzzy socks for his **mom;** a suspense novel, video game, and desk calendar for his **dad;** and a Barbie doll for his little sister.

Used instead of a conjunction such as 'and, but, or.'

- I spotted a lion at the **zoo; it** was sleeping on the grass.

Or

- I spotted a lion at the zoo, **and** it was sleeping on the grass.

Em Dash

An *em dash* is a versatile punctuation mark that can be used to replace commas, parentheses, colons, and semicolons. If you want to make a detail or fact stand out, an em dash can help. It's often used for emphasis and can signal a more conversational tone.

When used in pairs, the em dash sets off additional information not essential to the sentence. If you remove the dashes, the sentence still makes sense. For example:

- Regular exercise—such as walking, doing yoga, or riding a bike—is important for overall health.
- I ran into Mr. Hopkins—my grandmother's elderly neighbor—at the store.

Notice how commas or parentheses could have been used in these sentences instead:

- Regular exercise**, such as walking, doing yoga, or riding a bike,** is important for overall health.
- I ran into Mr. Hopkins **(my grandmother's elderly neighbor)** at the store.

Note: Parentheses, also called round brackets, are used more often in nonfiction than in fiction. They tend to jump out at the reader and can be annoying. For a sentence like the above examples, most editors advise setting off the extra information with commas or an em dash.

An em dash can also replace a colon that introduces additional information at the end of a sentence. For example:

- I bought my sister three gifts for her birthday—**perfume, a necklace, and earrings.**

Or

- I bought my sister three gifts for her birthday**: perfume, a necklace, and earrings.**

It can even replace a semicolon that connects two independent sentences.

- Sarah loved art **class—she** painted pictures to hang on the refrigerator.

Or

- Sarah loved art **class; she** painted pictures to hang on the refrigerator.

The em dash can also reveal an interruption or an abrupt change in tone. For example:

- "That guy stole my purse. I can't believe—" She broke off as the police officer approached.

How the em dash looks varies depending on the style guide. *In U.S. English, most guides recommend that the em dash be long and closed off with no spaces on either side.*

Several years ago—I can't remember how many—I moved into this neighborhood.

In UK English, it's more common for the dash to be shorter with a space on either side.

Several years ago – I can't remember how many – I moved into this neighborhood.

One more thing—use dashes sparingly. Too many on the page dilutes the effectiveness and can make your writing seem choppy.

Ellipses

The *ellipses*, a set of three periods, indicates the omission of words, a hesitation, or trailing off. Here are some examples:

- "Please . . . go away," she murmured.
- "I don't know what to make of this. It's just . . ."
- She paced the room, the phone to her ear. "No . . . we already donated last year . . . I'm really not interested."

How to format an ellipses depends on the style guide. The most accepted format is having a space before, between, and after the periods . . . like this. Some guides advise using four dots at the end of a sentence so that one can represent the period, like this . . . .

The key is to be consistent. Also, just like with the em dash, be sure not to overuse ellipses as too many will stick out to the reader. Some writers incorrectly use them instead of a comma to indicate a pause, or in place of an em dash to show an interruption.

Dialogue Punctuation

The final problem we'll discuss is dialogue punctuation. First, let's clarify the difference between dialogue and speech tags.

Dialogue is what's within the quotation marks. For example:

"Let's go to the movies."
"I'm bored."
"Want to go shopping?"

A *speech tag* is what's outside of the quotation marks such as *said, remarked, whispered, replied, hollered, murmured, bellowed,* or *answered.* For example:

"Let's go to the movies," **she suggested.**

"I could go for some popcorn," **Manuel said, studying the snack counter.**

"I'd like some candy," **his mother said.** "Something chocolate."

Here are some dialogue situations where beginners tend to make mistakes:

1. *Confusion often arises about whether to use a period or comma inside of a quotation mark.* In the above examples, notice how *she suggested*; *Manuel said, studying the snack counter*; and *his mother said* have become part of the original sentence. There is no hard stop between the dialogue and the speech tag; it's more of a soft pause, which is why we use a comma and not a period with speech tags.

When you're not using a speech tag, however, there *is* a hard stop at the end of the dialogue. It indicates the end of a sentence, which warrants a period. For example:

"I want a large popcorn with lots of **butter."**

"I want to get some candy**." John eyed the snack counter.**

"I've been wanting to see this movie for **ages."** She smiled.

Although *John eyed the snack counter* and *She smiled* show us who is speaking, they stand on their own as separate sentences. We should use a period inside the quotes to offset these supporting sentences from the dialogue.

2. *Question marks and exclamation points always go inside the quotes,* as in the following examples:

"Are you **okay?**"

"Are you **okay?**" he asked, frowning.

"Oh, **no!**"

"Oh, **no!**" he shouted.

3. *Learn when to capitalize pronouns in speech tags.* This is a common mistake:

"I can't wait to go to Florida next month**," She said.**

It doesn't make sense to capitalize *She* because, as we indicated earlier, the speech tag is part of the sentence.

> **Correct:** "I can't wait to go to Florida next month**," she said.**

If we flipped some words around, so that *She* started the sentence, then the capitalization would be correct. Just like with any other sentence, you would capitalize the first letter of the first word.

> **She said,** "I can't wait to go to Florida next month**."**

Typically, speech tags blend in better at the end of the dialogue, so use them at the beginning sparingly.

4. *Each speaker should get a new paragraph.* Every time someone speaks, show this by indenting and creating a new paragraph. This prevents large blocks of paragraphs, adds white space to the page, and helps to clarify who is talking. For example:

"Where in Florida are you going?" Jill asked.

"To St. Augustine. My parents have a place there in the winter." Monica scrolled through the photos on her phone. "Here's a picture of their condo."

Jill accepted the phone that Monica extended across the table. "Wow, it looks nice."

"Thanks."

5. *You can't grin, smile, frown, laugh, or shrug dialogue.* Grinning, smiling, frowning, laughing, shrugging, sighing, chuckling, etc. don't cause words to come out of your mouth. You might speak *and then* you grin, sigh, or laugh. We need that hard stop between sentences.

> **Incorrect:** "I can't wait until the kids open their presents on Christmas **morning,"** she grinned.
> **Correct:** "I can't wait until the kids open their presents on Christmas morning." **She grinned.**

6. *When a speaker's words in dialogue extend to more than one paragraph, use an opening quotation mark at the beginning of each paragraph.* Use a closing quotation mark, however, only at the end of the person's speech, not at the end of every paragraph. For example:

> "We had a great time on our trip, but it was a little stressful at first," Danielle said. "There was a tornado watch in the area after our flight landed. We were one of the last flights they allowed in. People in Florida must be used to this, because no one seemed rattled, but the sky looked ominous through the window and I didn't want to take a chance of getting caught in a **tornado.**

"Once we got our luggage and took care of the rental car, the kids and I bought snacks at the airport and waited until the watch period was over. Finally, we left and headed to the hotel."

"I would have done the same thing," Leslie said.

Tools To Make Grammar Easier

Every writer needs to be careful with grammar and punctuation, but it comes more easily to some people than others. Although you may still need to work with a copyeditor and proofreader, it's important to clean up your manuscript to the best of your ability before hiring anyone.

It can reduce paid rounds of copyediting if you catch the most obvious errors yourself. Also, it will be easier for a developmental editor and line editor to read your work and give you useful feedback if it's not filled with distracting punctuation mistakes. ***Developmental editors*, also called *content editors* or *structural editors*,** are typically the first type of editor to evaluate a manuscript. They look at the big picture and overall structure such as plot, characters, pacing, and description.

***Line editors*, sometimes known as *substantive editors*,** review a manuscript after the writer has done the rewrites from the developmental editing process. A line editor goes through each line to make the sentences flow more smoothly, honing in on overused words, sentence rhythm, and awkward phrasing.

Before working with a professional editor, always go into the spelling and grammar section of your writing software and run a spell check.

In Google Docs, go to Tools, Spelling and Grammar, Spelling and Grammar Check. In Microsoft Word, go to Review, Spelling and Grammar.

One warning: the spell check function has limitations and will only find a fraction of mistakes. If you used *their* but meant *there,* the spell check won't flag it as both words are in its dictionary.

If the spell check does flag a mistake, the suggested alternative may not be helpful. It's definitely worthwhile to run a scan, though, as the program will detect some errors and each one you fix will make the manuscript a little bit cleaner.

Second, check out editing software such as ProWritingAid, Grammarly, and AutoCrit. These tools go deeper than the built-in spell checks and can help you identify issues with capitalization, commas, periods, colons, semicolons, dashes, quotation marks, repeated words, passive voice, convoluted sentences, and lots more.

If cost is an issue, run your pages through the free versions of the software. You can mix and match; for example, do a scan through the free Grammarly and then one through the free AutoCrit. You might find a few more errors than if you had just used one tool.

It may also be worth investing in a paid version for more features. I always recommend ProWritingAid as I've used it myself for years and it seems to be the editing tool that gets the most rave reviews from authors.

When choosing which plan or which software to purchase, think about how often you'll use it. Are you a prolific author who churns out a couple of books per year? Then maybe a lifetime license would be a good investment. Paying a one-time fee for a lifetime license may be cheaper than renewing a subscription on an ongoing basis. However, if it takes you a long time to write a book and you only have one manuscript, then a short-term plan might be sufficient.

Just be aware that even paid grammar software doesn't replace a human copyeditor. While they have lots of benefits, electronic grammar checkers are known for flagging occasional correct punctuation and overlooking mistakes. They can help to make your manuscript more polished, but if you struggle with grammar and punctuation, then you'll want a copyeditor to evaluate your book once you've finished developmental editing and line editing.

In the meantime, work on improving your skills through the below resources. You'll discover articles, workshops, grammar and punctuation rules, quizzes, and more.

ProWritingAid.com

Grammarly.com

Autocrit.com

GrammarBook

Purdue University

Top 10 Countdown List

10. **Common nouns** are the generic name for a person, place, or thing in a class or group. For example: aunt, uncle, beach, building.

9. **Proper nouns** name an individual person, place, company, or organization and require capitalization. They can also refer to the titles of books, films, songs, and other media, e.g. Aunt Betty, Uncle John, Venice Beach.

8. The **Oxford Comma** is also called a serial comma and is the final comma in a list of three or more items. Although it is optional, the use of the serial comma needs to be consistent.

7. **Commas** represent a short pause and are used to divide parts of a sentence.

6. A **colon** is used to introduce a description, an explanation, or a list.

5. A **semicolon** is used between two parts of a sentence, usually when each part could form a grammatical sentence on its own. It shows a pause that is more pronounced than that indicated by a comma and can also separate the things in a list.

4. An **em dash** can be used to replace commas, parentheses, colons, and semicolons.

3. An ***ellipsis*** is a set of three periods indicating the omission of words, a hesitation, or trailing off.

2. ***Dialogue*** is what's within the quotation marks. A *speech tag* is what's outside of the quote marks such as *he said* or *she answered*.

1. ***Technology*** can help with grammar and punctuation. Tools include the spell check function in your writing software, ProWritingAid, Grammarly, and AutoCrit. Before hiring any type of editor, be sure to run a spell check and examine your manuscript for errors. *Developmental editors*, also called *content editors* or *structural editors*, are typically the first type of editor to evaluate a manuscript. They look at the big picture and overall structure such as plot, characters, pacing, and description. *Line editors*, sometimes known as *substantive editors*, review a manuscript after the writer has done the rewrites from the developmental editing process. Reading a manuscript riddled with mistakes can be distracting to these editors.

Meet Stacy Juba

Stacy Juba has written sweet and sassy chick lit novels, mysteries about determined women sleuths, and entertaining books for young adults and children. She has had novels ranked as #5 and #11 in the Nook Store and #30 on the Amazon Kindle Paid List.

Her books include the *Storybook Valley* chick lit series and the *Hockey Rivals* young adult sports novels. Stacy is also a freelance developmental editor, online writing instructor, and an award-winning journalist.

She is the founder of *Shortcuts for Writers*, and her signature course, *Book Editing Blueprint: A Step-By-Step Plan to Making Your Novels Publishable*, empowers fiction writers to think like an editor so they can save time and money.

She also runs the *Shortcuts for Writers: Editing Made Simple* group on Facebook.

Find out more about Stacy and her work at:

https://www.shortcutsforwriters.com/

https://www.facebook.com/profile.php?id=100057829702140

https://www.instagram.com/stacy_juba/

Critique Groups Offer Support, Guidance, and Friendship
Linda Rosen

How to Find One – How to Participate

Writing is a solitary endeavor. You sit alone in a room facing a computer screen—or a blank piece of paper. Maybe a dog or cat sleeps on the floor next to you and you lean down, now and then, to rub its furry head. They're your trusty companion, though mainly, you're alone. Your fictional characters may speak to you, insist they do this or that, yet they are not real. They're not truly your friends, no matter how many months you've spent with them. They aren't able to offer you support or guidance, cheer you on when you're frustrated, or celebrate when you sign that sought-after contract. And we writers need that. We need our cheerleaders. We need community. Being part of a critique group is one way of having that community—being with other writers, people with the same angst and anxieties you have. People who understand when you're thrilled with the words you've put together or understand when you're ready to throw your computer out the window and go fishing. These people are your community. No matter how many wonderful non-writer friends you have, or an adoring family, no one will understand you, "The Writer," as your group does.

So how do we find a critique group?

I found my original group from a Writers' Workshop I attended. It was my first foray into writing, and I was thrilled when someone in class suggested a few of us meet on another night to share our work and give each other feedback. We met at a quiet, out-of-the way table in a local Barnes and Noble. After getting coffee, tea, and some goodies—after all, we were going to be sitting there for a few hours— we **set up parameters** for the meeting: we would each have a maximum of ten minutes to read from our work-in-progress. Then we'd go around the table, giving each person a few minutes to critique.

First, and most importantly, we would each **start that critique with something positive**. Even if you feel the passage needs a ton of work, there is always something nice that can be said. Find it. Then, gently present your suggestions—what you think will help the writer accomplish her goal. And to that end, the **writer has to let the group know her goal at** the outset—the kind of feedback she's actually seeking for the pages presented. Keep in mind that all critiques are subjective. As in all writer's groups, there may be several opinions/suggestions on the same issue. That can be difficult for a writer. Which is correct? Which do I listen to? When members in my group disagree, and they definitely do sometimes, it makes me sit up straighter. I listen more closely to what each is saying, to glean what I can from the various comments rather than immediately tossing out the ones that don't sit well with me—as hard as that may be at times. I may not like what a group member says, but if it's offered **kindly**, as it always should be, I will consider it. And sometimes I surprise myself and find I agree with the critique. Or part of it.

Whether comments vary or everyone is in accord, each critique, as I said, needs to be given with kindness. Yet, unintentionally, some may hurt. Therefore, you must develop a **thick skin**. We all are sensitive when it comes to hearing opinions about our work. They're critiquing our book baby and we don't want anyone criticizing our children. Having that thick skin will help you sit quietly and **listen to all the comments and then decide which ones work for you**, which work for your vision. Then toss out the ones that don't. Of course, there will be times when you can't help but have an immediate reaction. You'll want to shout out, "No, I don't agree with that," or "No, you don't understand my character." It's happened to me and I do get my back up, though I stay quiet—or try to. It's not always easy, but it is best to not voice your opposition. **Do not get defensive.** It makes for a very uncomfortable atmosphere in the group and that is diametrically opposed to what we want. Remember the group is trying to help you, just as you will be attempting to help another member. Surprisingly, what's being said may just resonate with you a few hours later. It might make you go back and revise.

After a few years, my first critique group fell apart for all sorts of reasons. Some moved away. A few had given up writing. One woman realized varying opinions confused her and she'd rather work solely with her editor. We all have to do what works for us. I needed to find another group. I needed other ears to hear my words, to know if what I wanted to get across was coming across. Writers are too close to their own work to give it an honest, unbiased critique. And close friends and family aren't writers. They don't know the craft. They don't know what to suggest—how to make your story shine. But I didn't know how I was going to find a new group. At the time, I didn't have a network of writers. So I researched groups online and found TheNextBigWriter.com.

This online group was an entirely different experience than my in-person group. I never felt they were truly my tribe. We never connected. This was before Zoom took over our lives, when everything was in print. There was no personal contact. We read each other's words when they were uploaded to the site, and commented on those words, again, only in print. I did get some good feedback, but there was a great deal missing not being in person, not seeing each other face-to-face. Now an online group using Zoom or another live format can feel like an in-person group. I will have more on that later. For now, let's concentrate on non-visual writing groups, of which there are many. Here's a site that offers forty different groups, some with a fee, and some offering additional services such as workshops or newsletters.   https://thewritelife.com/find-a-critique-partner/ #But how do you find a critique partner or join a writing group. You might just find your group among these.

Most likely you will not form personal relationships with members of a non-visual online group unless you are extremely active in it and reach out to the other writers. Add not being able to see their faces and read visual cues, you may take what's being said the wrong way. Defensiveness can rear its ugly head. When part of an in-person group, a hard critique can be softened by a smile or tone of voice. That's not possible online. As with any critique, you have to be careful that **constructive criticism really does feel constructive**. That is more difficult when your critique is solely in writing. **Be conscious of the tone you use in your written feedback.**

The year I spent with TheNextBigWriter.com did help my writing, though even more it brought me to the New York City chapter of the Women's National Book Association (WNBA), which led me to my third critique group. One of the members of the online group recognized a movie theater I mentioned in my novel. She assumed I lived in the New York suburb near that theater and included information about the organization in her critique, suggesting I join. I researched WNBA and became a member. Immediately, I met many writers as well as other women in the book world: editors, agents, librarians, publicists, etc. Now I was networking, which all writers need to do.

But I will leave that topic for Book 3, which covers marketing. What I want to point out is that networking is another way of finding a critique group.

When searching for a group, look for one **that is homogeneous**. Novels encompass a great many genres. In general, anyone writing fiction should be adept at critiquing any type of fiction, though certain genres, such as mystery and romance, have specific tropes the writer must follow. Being a women's fiction writer, I do not know those specifics. And if I do, I'm not aware of it. Certainly, knowing the craft, I'd be able to give a constructive critique, yet I believe the romance or mystery writer would get better, possibly more specific feedback, from someone in their genre. The same goes for poetry. I don't know anything about poetry other than iambic pentameter, which I learned in high school. It would be a disservice for a poet to be in my critique group made up of fiction writers. Poets should find a group of like-minded writers, just as memoirists might find it more comfortable being with others pouring their personal stories onto the page.

The critique group that formed from friends I made at WNBA helped me write my debut novel. They peppered me with questions about the protagonist's wants and desires and made me dig deeper into my character with their pro and con comments. In addition to pointing out little inconsistencies in the pages I read to them, such as a character having curly hair on one page and straight on another, they looked at the bigger picture—my protagonist was too cold. They did not have sympathy for her and that was not what I wanted. I wanted my readers to connect, to recognize themselves in her, even tear-up in certain scenes. I was guilty of what I wrote earlier. Defensiveness. I was not at all happy with their comments. After I learned to bite my tongue, I did what was right. I listened, even if I wanted to argue. Then I pondered their words, which were all given **sensitively**, and digested them. Ultimately, I agreed and revised. And I was so glad to have this group who understood what my story needed, and what *I* needed. They hadn't simply listened to the words I read, they took my story seriously, as if it were their own, and helped me make it better. That's what we want in a critique group. And from experience, I can say that comes from making personal, meaningful connections with the people in the group. They can become true friends. Your writing family, in short, your "tribe." At the minimum, they know your story and can help make it shine.

Snow and ice affected my critique group. Not that we couldn't continue taking the train into Manhattan, as we had every week—it was that two of us didn't want to spend winters in the north anymore. We were at a point in our lives when we could go south for six months. Because this was before Zoom, the group had to disband for the winter. Both of us "snowbirds" found other critique groups in Florida, made up of other snowbirds as well as full-timers. I'll get to that soon. Now, I want to focus on why the New York group stuck together, if only in spring and summer, for several more years. We depended on each other. Our stories were better for it. Our characters were more developed. Yes, we could have continued sharing pages via email or Google Drive during the winter months when two of us were in Florida, and sometimes we did. But being in person is what we needed. Sitting around a dining room table, or one in a quiet corner of The Hyatt at Grand Central Station, lent itself to much more discussion than typing a critique and sending it into cyberspace. The give and take of ideas and concerns flow much more easily in person. When you share your messy rough drafts with someone, you are giving a peek into a deep part of yourself. You're vulnerable, letting someone into your angst, anxieties, and insecurities, as well as your joys. Those connections are strong. The group hasn't only helped with your writing, it has, hopefully, made your life richer. And it's hard to give that up.

Networking, again, played its part in finding my Florida critique group. As of this writing, we have been together for seven years and have no plans to stop. We started in-person meetings once a week in each other's homes. We brought our own lunch, but the hostess always had drinks and snacks. For some reason, M&Ms go down very well while discussing characters and plot points. We tried meeting every other week but found we preferred the weekly feedback. Lou, one of the members, says she needs the deadline to keep her focused, to keep her writing. And Carren says the weekly feedback keeps her moving forward with her story. So **show up!** Even if you don't have pages to read, and there will be times that you won't. Life can get in the way. Or maybe, even better, your manuscript is with the editor and you haven't started on your next book. Come to the meeting anyway. Be respectful of everyone else's needs and you can use your allotted group time to talk about ideas for your next book, or for marketing your upcoming novel. The group is here to help in all aspects of your writing journey. Everyone is depending on you. They're anxious for your feedback. And, you may glean something from the day's discussion. Pat, another member of my group, says she learns from each of the critiques. Even when not directly related to her work, she picks up strands of advice or knowledge she can use.

The advice/suggestion/critique you give can come in the form of character development, plot point, any aspect of the craft, even tiny tidbits related to the scene. I once pointed out to a writer friend that she had her character on the wrong New York subway to get to her intended destination. Anyone reading the book, knowing the subway system, would be annoyed. And that is not what we want to do to our readers. Yet the writer, if alone, would have kept that mistake, and maybe her editor wouldn't have picked it up either. It was a tidbit, but those little bits, or what my group calls little-littles, help make a story shine.

We all have knowledge and experiences we bring to our writing. We bring the same to our critiques, helping our writer friends make their scenes, settings, and characters more realistic. A bit of advice I was once given, and that stays with me and everyone in my critique group, came from the sole man in our group, Joe. My story was inspired by a true story, yet the group kept telling me one of my plot points was not working. It was flat. The reader would not be engaged, would not care, in fact readers probably wouldn't even like my protagonist. I argued that the incident actually happened. It was real. And Joe said, "Don't dick up a good story with the truth." Excuse my French, I just had to use his exact words. It's exactly why the phrase has stuck with me and with everyone in my group. Think about it. Real life doesn't necessarily work in fiction. We have to engage our readers and Joe, very succinctly, told me how to do it. I was writing fiction so that's what I did. Fictionalized. And the story was much better for it.

Earlier, I wrote that I would "talk" about online, in-person critique groups. These virtual writers' groups are a more recent way of finding your community. Networking through writing organizations such as The Women's National Book Association, Women Fiction Writers Association, Romance or Mystery Writers of America, American Pen Women, etc. are good resources for finding a group. Now, with a selection of virtual sites (some may be in the link I provided above), geography doesn't have to stop us from finding writing partners— whether a group of six, eight, or only two.

The Covid-19 pandemic, which forced us all to stay at home, brought my Florida writers' group to Zoom. As of this writing, we are meeting virtually every Tuesday afternoon. And since some of us are snow-birds, it doesn't matter what part of the world we live in. We meet in every season. A former member who had dropped out of the group when she moved away has joined us again.

Because we are on Zoom, we are still able to see each other and read the expressions on the faces as members critique, which, as I said earlier, is very important. Though just as easy as it is to see smiles or glints in an eye, we're able to spot boredom or disinterest. When a group meets in person, it's rare for one of the members to walk away from the table or answer a phone. In fact, answering a call, unless it's an emergency, is a huge no-no. **All cell phones are turned off or put on silent mode during the meeting.** Unfortunately, one member, let's call her J, did not heed that rule once we started meeting online. We had to constantly remind her to mute, since she refused to turn her phone off. J also had occasionally given curt, harsh critiques when we met in person. They happened more often on Zoom. Was it that she felt being in the privacy of her own home, not in another member's, she could do whatever she wanted? I'll never understand her motives, other than she only seemed interested in what we could do for her. She was no longer, if she ever had been, part of the community we'd formed. Sadly, we had to have a private meeting to discuss J's behavior and eventually asked her to leave. This is not something you want to happen in a critique group, but if there is a member who is souring the pot, ask her nicely to leave. Explain the issues yet stay firm. It's not easy, but it must be done. Critique groups are supportive. Everyone in the group must be so, or they don't belong.

There are various ways to present work in a critique group. I know of one writer who left her group because she felt pressure having to read pages sent to her each week by members of her group. She was supposed to read all ten pages from each member and be ready to critique when they met in person. Ten pages may not seem a lot, but when they're coming from five, six, or seven people, they add up. It takes away from your own writing time and your own personal reading time. Another group I know of presents pages when they meet in person. Members are supposed to read along silently when the writer reads her excerpt. That's perfect for those who work better visually. Personally, I find that distracting. My group tried it but I found myself correcting errors on the page rather than listening to what was being read aloud. For me, reading for ten minutes max, while the group listens, works perfectly. Any longer and my mind wanders. Plus, we want to leave enough time to discuss the pages and not be on Zoom for too many hours. We have found, with six people, three hours is what we need. Each group will decide for themselves. Make sure you are comfortable with the parameters. If not, **speak up**. You may not be the only one objecting. Don't let one person take over. Critique groups are just that—a group.

Participation

Now that you have your group, where are you going to meet? If online, that's easy. You can stay in your pajamas in your own home. But if you meet in person, where will you go? Meeting in each other's homes works nicely. It's cozy, but make sure you don't overstay your welcome. When the group time is over, unless the host asks you to stay, pack up your things and head home. My group has also met in hotel restaurants, during off hours. As long as you keep ordering, they don't mind you taking up a table. I know of several other groups that have met, in warm weather, outside at Starbucks. A really fun place to meet, if you're in the New York City area, is The Algonquin hotel. You can channel Dorothy Parker, George S. Kaufman, Harpo Marx and the others of the famous Algonquin Round Table. My group met there many times over the summer months when we snowbirds were back in New York and we had our own round table! But if you're in a public place, you must keep your voice down when reading aloud. There was one time I was reading a very sexy scene from the novel I was working on. I thought my voice was low. There were only one or two other tables occupied, and they were far enough away. But suddenly a hush came over the room. The silence hung like fog. Everyone was listening. I looked up, smiled, giggled, then lowered my voice even more. No other critique was needed. It was obvious the scene worked!

There are no doubt reasons, other than those I've posed, that you might have when making your decision to join a critique group. At a minimum, being part of one is enjoyable. You just have to find the group that fits. Ultimately, you will have a community that understands "Writer You." You'll become a better communicator and, hopefully, since that's the goal, a better storyteller. Everything you glean from the critiques, even the suggestions you toss aside, will positively influence your work when you're back in your office sitting alone in front of your computer.

Top Ten Points to Finding and Participating in Critique Groups

10. Network through organizations and social media writing and reading groups to find an in-person homogenous group, or to start one.

9. Research online critique groups, if this suits you better than in-person.

8. Set parameters for group sessions, including time allotments and the number of pages to read/submit. Speak up to let your preferences be known.

7. Let the group know if you have anything specific you'd like help with on a particular meeting day.

6. Always start your critique with positive feedback.

5. Always give constructive criticism and give it kindly. We writers are vulnerable, be sensitive.

4. Develop tough skin.

3. Don't be defensive. Stay quiet while your work is being critiqued.

2. Listen closely to all critiques, then decide what works for your vision. Remember, critiques are subjective.

1. Show up! Even if you don't have pages to share.

Meet Linda Rosen

Fitness Professional turned novelist, Linda Rosen's books are set in the "not-too-distant past" and examine how women reinvent themselves despite obstacles thrown their way. A central theme is that blood is not all that makes a family– and they always feature a piece of jewelry!

Her novels, *The Disharmony of Silence, Sisters of the Vine,* and the upcoming, *The Emerald Necklace* are published by Black Rose Writing. In addition to writing novels, Linda was a contributor to *Women in the Literary Landscape: A WNBA Centennial Publication* for the Women's National Book Association.

She is a member of the Women's Fiction Writers Association and co-founder of the South Florida chapter of the Women's National Book Association where she holds the position of VP of Programming. In addition, Linda is a founding member of *The Author Talk Network* and an administrator of the Facebook Group, *Bookish Road Trip,* editor of their newsletter "Wanderlust."

Linda lives with her husband in New Jersey, but when the leaves fall and she has to swap sandals for shoes and socks, they move to their home in Florida.

Find out more about Linda and her work at:

https://www.linda-rosen.com/

https://www.facebook.com/lindarosenauthor/

https://www.instagram.com/lindarosenauthor/

Three Things a Publishing Gatekeeper Wants

Janyre Tromp

You've spent months researching and writing. You have a proposal gathered together and a full novel written. Now your goal is to gain the attention of an editor or agent.

The problem is that the gatekeepers receive hundreds of proposals a month. By necessity, agents and editors often approach proposals looking for reasons to quickly weed out and narrow down the choices in their inbox. The good news is that if you can make it through the first triage, you're well on your way to a contract . . . or at least a request for more information. But how do you get past the first cut?

With nearly twenty-five years of evaluating manuscripts for a traditional publisher and five years working as a novelist myself, I'm often asked for advice regarding surviving the first purge. The good news is that there are three characteristics you can adopt that will help you make the cut.

Be Knowledgeable

Let's be honest, as much as we all want to write and publish the books we want to, I also like getting a paycheck so I can feed my kids. And so do all the other agents and editors out there. That means finding authors who are professionals . . . who want to make money, too.

Agents/editors combine the pitch for your book with your comparables, bio, and platform to assess how serious you are. Here's how you can help yourself.

Know the Market

Your first step in showing you're a professional shows up in your pitch. Monitor the market for what sells and what might sell in the future and pitch that.

In the industry, we often refer to the salability of a book as a hook, and it is almost always the first thing an agent or editor looks at. If your one-sentence pitch fails to hook us and draw us in, we'll reject a proposal without reading further.

You can find your hook several ways. Pay attention to what's selling. Also, understand that traditional publishing works at least three years out. Don't plan on an old trend holding and don't pitch a hook that will take place six months from now.

Beyond that, you can try your hand at forecasting what might be interesting in a few years. What major movies are coming (check the listings at IMDb.com)? What sporting events are coming and where will they take place? What anniversaries (one-hundred-year anniversaries of wars, fifty-year anniversaries of major cultural events, etc.) are coming in the next three to four years? What is something that might affect what people are interested in? Whatever it is, write about that and then tell the editor/agent why the topic will appeal.

Asian characters became a huge focus after the 2018 Olympics. Lighthearted books uplifted spirits during the stay home orders. Realistic books with magical elements have their roots in the oppressed people of Latin America during the 1960s, but there's been a resurgence, perhaps partly attributed to the pandemic, partly to continued oppression of minority groups, and partly (at least in my mind) because of the popularity of movies in the genre.

In general, look at upcoming or current issues and think about how your audience will react or what they might think about . . . which takes us to the next thought.

(A side note for authors pitching a second or third contract. You might need to change with the market. Being willing to do so shows you're flexible and willing to do what it takes.)

Know Your Reader

All the research in the world won't help you if your readers don't care. The first step to making sure you have a book that will interest your reader is to start with defining who your reader is. Use psychographics (attitudes and desires) rather than demographics (age, location, and sex). What are the issues your reader cares about? What are they interested in? What do they struggle with? Does your style fit what your reader reads?

If you are the expert on your reader, be sure to show the agent/editor not only why your book appeals in general, but why your readers in specific will line up to buy your book. The best way to tackle this is to use comparable titles to show that your style and topic fits and yet are different enough from everything else out there.

When an editor/agent reads, "There's no book out there like mine," we interpret that as you either don't know the market or there is no market. Trust me, if there are alien vampire Amish books on the market, there's something on the market similar to your book. Your job is to find it.

Know Who You're Pitching

While it might be common sense, it's important enough to point out: every agent/editor is looking for something distinct. They have a variety of preferences, different gaps in their lists, distinct requirements, etc. Your job here is to know as much about your target gatekeeper as you can without being a stalker.

Your book may be fantastic, but not for a specific publisher. And you may have the next fantasy bestseller, but you don't want an agent who specializes in historicals. They simply don't have the contacts you need.

Save your heart from an immediate disheartening rejection by doing your homework ahead of time. Check the current *Writer's Market Guide* to start with, then move to websites. Look at what other books the editor acquires, or the agent represents. Does their list complement your manuscript? Or is your book completely different or, worse yet, is there a book that would directly compete? Or grab a book you love, search online for the author's agent (sometimes it's listed on the copyright page), note their publisher, and tailor your pitch from there. Make an effort to hang out with gatekeepers on social media or at a writer's conference. We're people. We like to help people we enjoy.

Also, a note here. Agents/editors will check your social media accounts. If we see complaints about agents, editors, other authors, etc., we'll assume you're difficult to work with and will pass on your work. The publishing world is small. Do your best to not burn a bridge and definitely don't explode it in public.

Know How to Talk to Your Reader

The industry often refers to how and where an author talks to their reader as an author's platform. Before you panic, building a platform isn't all about numbers, though they do come into play. It's about showing you have the ability, desire, and wherewithal to reach your audience. If you're a writer, you want to talk to readers. Yes?

So go where your audience is (bookstores, Bookstagram, BookTok, Facebook, libraries, blogs, podcasts, etc.) and talk to them . . . before you have a book. Ask what you can contribute or give to the audience that would benefit them. Create a newsletter magnet and build a list. Talk to them about the things you love. For me, it's books, my crazy animals, and nature. And you know what? Those things appear in my books. So folks who like my social media or newsletter will (surprise, surprise) like my books.

Showing an editor/agent that you are already talking to your readers shows you know what you're doing. Your targeted gatekeeper is more apt to trust you to know what you're talking about and can sell a few books, which is ultimately what we all want.

Being a professional is only one characteristic you need in order to stand out.

Be Sparkly

With my apologies for my unusual word choice, a book also needs to have that something hard-to-describe that sets it apart. This does not mean you need to decorate your proposal in literal sequins or have an outgoing personality. Being sparkly is the intangible thing that makes your manuscript a work of art rather than a nice waiting room picture.

The acquisitions process is uniquely personal and requires an agent/editor to fall in love. And for that to happen, you have to go back to the stale relationship advice you got in high school and college. You have to be yourself . . . but still work on improving. Here are a few things you can work on in order to increase the chance that your book sparks the flames of a gatekeeper's love.

Find and Embrace Your Style

Eventually, you want someone to be able to pick up one of your books and say, "Hey, I know who wrote this." That doesn't mean your books all sound the same or are boring. It just means that a reader knows what makes a book yours, as well as what sets you apart from others.

My books are described as lyrical historical suspense or women in tough historical situations who are stronger than they think they are. James Patterson is known for his thrillers. Stephen King for his brilliantly plotted horror. Emily Henry for her light beach reads. And Margaret Atwood for her searing social commentary hidden behind worlds built in a way you want to look away from but can't.

I realize finding your style is easier said than done. I've been there. One of the best pieces of advice I can give you is to study other writers inside and outside your own genre. Take notes. Notice how they create tension and amp up emotions. Pay attention to how an author tells a story (how they use point of view (POV), hold and tell secrets, etc.) and build characters.

And then do something similar without copying. Trust me, an editor/agent will recognize the difference between echoes and mimicry. Instead, note how Stephen King slows down a scene to create tension or Mimi Matthews uses a single word to create a zing of attraction, and borrow the technique for your own writing. But make it your own.

How? The best way to find your voice is to write. Writers are never not writing. Keep a notebook by your bed with a pen with a built-in light. Use Aqua Notes (waterproof paper) in the shower. Take advantage of the voice-to-text on your phone. Be constantly writing. Test bits out on your audience. See what they react to. It's one of the best ways to keep a platform moving and interesting.

Make Your Opening Pages Work For You

There's something special about first impressions and love at first sight. Make your opening line something that makes the agent/editor intrigued or dumbfounded, that somehow encapsulates where your character is headed.

That first line is important, but don't panic. Most professional editors/agents will read beyond an okay first line. That said, if the first page is clunky or not on target, that's a gatekeeper's excuse to eliminate one of the projects cluttering their inbox.

If it takes a bit of time to get into your groove, cut pages to move the groove to the beginning.

Sometimes it Isn't You

Just like some relationships don't work because of timing or the other party's bad mood, what makes a proposal catch fire is its sparkle. You can do all the things right and it just doesn't work, or it's simply not the right time.

I have, more than once, let an author know I couldn't do a book at a certain time, but then went back a year or two later to acquire the book (my favorite of which might be *The Unlikely Yarn of the Dragon Lady* by Sharon Mondragon).

But you throw all that work out the window if your book falls apart in the small things.

Be Detail-Oriented

If you know me, you know I love my job—reading for a living is the best job in the world. So you'd think my favorite part of being a writer is the editing. But it isn't.

As a writer, I'm an unorganized, inconsistent, rabbit-trailing disaster —my editor-self's worst nightmare. But as an editor, I know details are the cornerstone to creating a book readers enjoy, agents accept, and acquisitions editors buy.

What's a novelist to do?

Make the following lists, even if it's after the fact. They'll help you find anything that's incomplete or not quite working.

And, for the record, your friendly acquisitions editor or potential agent is probably going to ask for some of these lists anyway. You might as well do it now when you have time to fix any potential issues that crop up.

Make an Annotated Timeline or Calendar

I often say that an annotated outline is the most powerful tool in first-round, substantive edits. Why?

A timeline helps you make sure that it snows in January not August (at least if you're in the Midwest of the United States). Or that your character who dies in Chapter 6 doesn't reappear in Chapter 12.

A timeline also helps you identify problems with backstory. In addition to including when you reveal backstory within your main timeline, you might also consider creating a separate timeline with all your backstory in chronological order. That way, you can make sure that, when a character does something at nine-years-old and then something else five years later, your character is fourteen and not eleven.

Trust me, details matter like a big hole in a canvas matters.

But most importantly, creating a timeline helps you check your structure. Having everything laid out reveals if you've missed something in the development of a character or plot point and makes sure your plot doesn't drag or rush. You should clearly see the rise and fall of action.

So how do you do it?

Creating a timeline is relatively easy (if time consuming) to do. Basically, you go through each chapter noting what happens and when.

Before you panic, both MS Word and Scrivener have ways to create outlines. You use header styles in MS Word and scene names and the synopsis in the Inspector in Scrivener. If you use those functions as you write, you'll have ready-made timelines. Or you can go through and create the timeline as you edit.

Make a List of Themes

Really a theme is the answer to the question: what is your book about? Like friendship in *The Lord of the Rings* or the power of unconditional love in Francine Rivers's *Redeeming Love*.

If the answer to the question is muddy, you might have a rewrite on your hands. If you aren't sure what your themes are, ask yourself what your book is about, what your characters are struggling with, and how they deal with their struggles. You'll likely find your themes inside those questions.

If not, the good news is that it isn't unusual for themes to become clear partway through writing a book. As you create your main book outline, you should start seeing ideas, themes, and repeated concepts throughout your manuscript. Use a different color font and add the themes to your outline.

This will ensure that there is the whisper of your major themes at the beginning of your book. Whatever happens at the end of your book must have the pieces introduced at the beginning.

But a theme outline will also help you track if you've let important arcs drop.

Make a List of Characters

All the cool events in the world can't make an interesting book on their own. You need characters that fit particular roles. And that's where your list of characters comes in.

To create one, simply list your main characters and primary side characters, then note who they are as well as their function in the book. Make sure to pay special attention to your antagonist (whether that's an internal conflict or an external villain or force). Novels live and die by the character or force who creates tension.

So, for example, in *The Lord of the Rings,* Sam is a sidekick and Gandalf the Grey is a mentor.

Once you have the basics down, write out each character's basic physical description as well as their greatest fear, their goal, and what motivates them.

This practice will reveal overlaps. Do you have two mentor characters? Or maybe two sidekick characters. If so, you need to consider deleting one or combining them. A good editor will immediately see overlap and wonder what other elements are flabby in the manuscript.

Then check for inconsistencies. Does Betty Jo have blonde hair on page ten and curly red hair on page one hundred ten? Or more subtly, does Betty Jo have a control-freak complex in Chapter 1 and let people run all over her without saying anything in Chapter 10?

Or you might find an underdeveloped character. Sometimes, as you're writing out who these people are, you might realize that you've created a caricature. A villain who has no reason to do what he does. Or a hero who is practically perfect in every way. If you find these things before you send them to me, you can go in and fine tune your characters to make them stand out in the crowd.

Make a List of Overused Words

One of the best ways to sharpen your writing is to be purposeful in word choice. I keep a list of words I tend to overuse. Before I turn in any piece of writing (including this essay), I search for my seventy-five pesky terms (you can download my list here:

http://beautifuluglyme.com/janyres-75-secret-search-words/).   And then every project seems to grow its own special words. (I once used the word shiny thirty times in a manuscript).

The idea isn't to eliminate the words, but to use them with purpose. If you can make an agent/editor sigh at how you caress a beautiful word, you'll be well on your way to winning them over.

Of course, there is no guaranteed path to publication, but if you work to become knowledgeable, sparkly, and detail-oriented, you'll be well on your way to standing out from the pack.

Before You Hit Submit - 10 Things to Do Before Pitching

10. Pick a saleable topic & genre.

As a debut author, you'll have the best chance of being picked up if you follow genre rules and pick a topic that appeals to your target market.

9. Finish your manuscript.

The best thing for your career is to type THE END. No agent or editor will contract a novelist without a complete manuscript. Make sure you're following genre rules for content and length.

8. Make contacts.

While you're writing, be a good community member. Support other authors and the reading community.

7. Write a hook (and then test drive it with the target audience).

Writing a one-sentence summary may be the hardest part of being an author. But it's crucial to catching the attention of the publishing gatekeepers.

6. Make sure your first page catches attention.

Most successful authors rewrite their first page multiple times. Don't worry about having it perfect until after you've finished the rest of your manuscript. Then find the point in the story that catches attention without being too confusing.

5. Do your homework on the agent or editor.

Know what genres the agent or editor is or is not looking for. Don't pitch a book that is too similar to something they already have. But do pay attention to complementary titles.

4. Put together a proposal that fulfills noted requirements.

Every agent I'm familiar with has a list of what they're looking for in a proposal. Don't be cute with fonts. Times New Roman (or similar serif font) 12 pt., double-spaced is typical. Follow what the agent requests and then trust your agent to put together a proposal editors will appreciate.

3. Show you know the industry with comparable titles.

Comparable titles should be three years old or newer. The point is to show the salability of your topic and your style.

2. Edit and proofread. Then edit some more.

Remember that agents and editors receive hundreds of manuscripts. We're looking for people that will do the work.

1. Submit through the proper channels and in the requested format.

It is rare for an agent to accept pitches via social media and even more rare for an editor to do so. Pitching on social media is likely to be ignored.

Meet Janyre Tromp

Janyre Tromp is a firm believer in the power of an entertaining story. As such, she is an acquisitions and developmental editor for Kregel Publications with twenty-five years of industry experience.

And at night, she is a historical novelist who loves spinning tales that, at their core, hunt for beauty, even when it isn't pretty. Her books (*Shadows in the Mind's Eye, O Little Town,* and *It's a Wonderful Christmas*) have been described as lyrical suspense and are available wherever books are sold. And all that happens from her unfinished basement surrounded by her family, two crazy cats, and slightly eccentric Shetland Sheepdog.

You can hang out with her online on most social media platforms and she has a free novella available on her website.

You can find out more about Janyre and her work at:

https://beautifuluglyme.com/

https://www.facebook.com/groups/janyresreadinginsiders

https://www.instagram.com/JanyreTromp/

http://JanyreTromp.com (where you can grab a copy of her FREE novella, *Wide Open*)

Afterword

This book, and the two that follow, grew out of a sense of urgency to share information and uplift authors. I've written four books and many articles. Still, I learn. I started out as a non-fiction writer. There was no TBR, WIP, POV, plotters or pantsers, or the myriad of other terms and acronyms that needed to be mastered. There was no need for a social media presence, or beta readers, or book coaches, or marketing plans. Even "craft," as we discussed it here, was not a focus of my work. Adverbs were still okay. When I wrote my novel, *The Eves*, all that, and my life, changed.

I am a writer, entrepreneur, and radio host of The Storytellers. The latter all because of my novel. Writing books, as Emma Dhesi says, changes us. Just under a year ago I went to my friend and colleague Mary Helen Sheriff of the Bookish Road Trip and said, "I have an idea for a new radio show and marketing plan that celebrates book release and the authors that create them." I received an immediate "I'm in!" I then consulted with friend and radio station owner Pam Stack of Authors on the Air Global Radio Network. Pam is a visionary who supports authors. LAUNCH PAD was born—just four months from idea to first episode. Goal set, goal met.

However, just a few episodes in, it occurred to me that many of our guests, seasoned writers or novices, all were talking craft—what they knew, what they didn't, and what they wished they knew when they published their first books. (Lightbulb!) Enter Stephanie Larkin, CEO of Red Penguin Books and Scottish-based Book Coach, Emma Dhesi. I danced the idea of a three-part book series in front of them and Mary; and well, to use launch pad terminology, we had lift off!

I am incredibly excited about this series—the information and wisdom included, the enthusiasm and the process of collaboration shared across continents, the vision to get these books out into the hands of authors within less than a year from idea to print, and the opportunity to uplift the writing community the same way I have been uplifted by it.

One last note. We have included names, bios, websites, and contact information for each of our contributors. In Linda Rosen's chapter on critique groups, she focused on how they offer support, guidance and friendship. We hope this book just expanded your group of guides and friends. We genuinely encourage you to reach out and continue the dialogue with any of us. It is together that we soar.

Thank you for joining us at the Launch Pad the Countdown to Writing Your Book. From Amy Ferris' inspirational opening words to simply write words, through each of the chapters, countdowns, and planning sheets, we hope you have gained the skills, insights, and support to have your work take flight!

We look forward to, and encourage, your journey! We will look for you in books two and three on publishing and marketing. Take off with us!

Sarasota, Florida

February 2023

www.gracesammon.net on IG and FB I'm at GraceSammonWrites

Next Steps

We are so excited to join you on your writing journey. For more free resources and downloads, please visit https://launchpadcountdown.com/downloads-1/

and enter the password LaunchPadWriting.

Be sure to grab your copy of:

Available April 25, 2023

Available June 20, 2023

Available wherever books are sold.